From the East Gate

From the East Gate

A Preaching Anthology, 1996–2024

ADAM S. LINTON

WIPF & STOCK · Eugene, Oregon

FROM THE EAST GATE
A Preaching Anthology, 1996–2024

Copyright © 2025 Adam S. Linton. All rights reserved. Except for brief quotations in critical publications or reviews, no part of this book may be reproduced in any manner without prior written permission from the publisher. Write: Permissions, Wipf and Stock Publishers, 199 W. 8th Ave., Suite 3, Eugene, OR 97401.

Wipf & Stock
An Imprint of Wipf and Stock Publishers
199 W. 8th Ave., Suite 3
Eugene, OR 97401

www.wipfandstock.com

PAPERBACK ISBN: 979-8-3852-6583-1
HARDCOVER ISBN: 979-8-3852-6584-8
EBOOK ISBN: 979-8-3852-6585-5

VERSION NUMBER 122925

New Revised Standard Version Bible, copyright © 1989 National Council of the Churches of Christ in the United States of America. Used by permission. All rights reserved worldwide.

Revised Standard Version of the Bible, copyright © 1946, 1952, and 1971 by the National Council of the Churches of Christ in the United States of America. Used by permission. All rights reserved worldwide.

New International Version, copyright © 1973, 1978, 1984, 2011 by Biblica, Inc. Used with permission. All rights reserved worldwide.

Revised English Bible, copyright © 1989 by Cambridge University Press and Oxford University Press. All rights reserved.

To Lori,
my wife,
and our children,
Christina, Rebecca, Patrick, Sarah, and Hope

"Though for no other cause, yet for this; that posterity may know we have not loosely through silence permitted things to pass away as in a dream."

—Richard Hooker, *The Laws of Ecclesiastical Polity*, Preface, Chapter i.1[1]

"Nothing in the world is harder than speaking the truth, and nothing is easier than flattery."

—Fyodor Dostoevsky, *Crime and Punishment*, Part Six, Chapter IV[2]

"A work that aspires, however humbly, to the condition of art should carry its justification in every line . . . My task which I am trying to achieve is, by the power of the written word, to make you hear, to make you feel—it is, before all, to make you see. That—and no more, and it is everything. If I succeed, you shall find there everything according to your deserts; encouragement, consolation, fear, charm—all you demand; and, perhaps, also that glimpse of truth for which you have forgotten to ask."

—Joseph Conrad, *Narcissus,* Preface[3]

"All honor to relevance, but pastors should be good marksmen who aim their guns beyond the hill of relevance."

—Karl Barth, *Homiletics*, Chapter 3, "Actual Preparation of the Sermon," III.2.c[4]

"It pleased God by the foolishness of preaching to save them that believe."

—Paul the Apostle, *The First Epistle to the Corinthians*, 1:21, KJV

"Ye are not brought unto God by us, but by Him. Even though we do these things, we have not undertaken a work of our own, but His."

—John Chrysostom, *Homilies on Colossians* [1:24][5]

---

1. Hooker, *Works of Richard Hooker*, 1:125.
2. Dostoevsky, *Brothers Karamazov* (Garnett). See Dostoevsky, *Brothers Karamazov*, 476 (Pevear and Volokhonsky).
3. Conrad, *Secret Sharer*, 139, 141.
4. Barth, *Homiletics*, 118–19.
5. Chrysostom, *Homilies on Colossians* 4 (*NPNF*1 13:276).

Contents

Preface—Holy Scripture: What It Is and How to Read It | ix
Introduction | xix

"From the East Gate" | 1
"Which Adam?" | 5
"The Binding of God?" | 10
"The Benefit of Knowing That We Are Sinners" | 14
"The Table with the Open Space" | 21
"But We See Jesus" | 26
"The Taste for Heaven" | 31
"Stretched" | 37
"The Merchant and the Pearl" | 41
"On This Day the Lord Has Acted" | 46
"No Cross Is So Extreme, as to Have None" | 51
"Love Bears All Things" | 57
"Christ Became a Curse for Us" | 64
"Grant Us, O Lord, to Trust in You with All Our Hearts" | 68
"Rivers of Living Water" | 75
"Wages or Free Gift" | 81
"Puddleglum's Testimony" | 86
"Strive to Be Found by Him at Peace" | 90
"Dear One, I Say to You, Arise" | 96
"Listen, Then See" | 101
"Approach the Throne" | 106

"And He Must Win the Battle" | 111
"The Banquet of Consequence" | 115
"Blessed Is the Man" | 119
"God Is Reigning from the Tree" | 125
"The Surpassing Value" | 128
"Something Else" | 134
"Receive the Kingdom of God as a Little Child" | 138

Biographical Note | 145
Bibliography | 147
Scripture Index | 151

Preface

Holy Scripture: What It Is and How to Read It

ἀλλ' ὅμως τὸ ἐν τῇ ἔξω σοφίᾳ τέλειον
τῆς νηπιώδους τοῦ θείου λόγου διδασκαλίας ἐστὶ μικρότερον.[1]

Letting the Bible Speak to Us

THE ORDINATION OATH IN the Episcopal Church includes the following: "I solemnly declare that I do believe the Holy Scriptures of the Old and New Testaments to be the Word of God, and to contain all things necessary to salvation."[2]

And Karl Barth wrote: "[The] most debatable and least assimilable parts" of Scripture are "more important than the best and most necessary things that we ourselves have said or can say."[3]

Of course, neither the Oath nor Barth requires of us wooden literalisms or narrow, simplistic interpretations. We must allow the books of Scripture—in all their variety, all their layers of meaning, in all their

---

1. "That which is perfect in this world's wisdom is less than the most childlike teaching of the divine Word." Gregory, *Homilies on the Song of Songs* 1, J.35.

2. *Book of Common Prayer*, 513, 526, 538.

3. Barth, *Church Dogmatics* 1/2:266 (section 21.2, "Freedom Under the Word," of the fifth fascicle of the T&T Clark Study Edition, found in the second fascicle of the first English language edition of the *Dogmatics* on p. 719). I am well aware of Barth's qualified (and complicated) reticence to state quite as boldly (and as simply), as the Ordination Declaration does, that the Holy Scriptures *are* the Word of God. This is a reticence that I do not share, although I certainly appreciate Barth's concerns. See, however, Barth, *Church Dogmatics* 1/2, sections 19–21, especially section 19.2, "Scripture as the Word of God."

challenges, their paradoxes and their clarities, and in their various genres—to speak to us on their own terms.

In my own Bible study and teaching, I devote almost all of my attention to the canonical texts as they are. To be sure, there's often some important background information to consider. But one thing I make a point of avoiding is spending too much time on conjectures of what came before the texts of the canonical Scriptures. Such conjectures often tell us much more about those who make them than the texts ostensibly being studied.

A Sacramental Approach to Bible Study

Rather, I seek to foster a sacramental experience of the Bible: the Scriptures as the instrument of living encounter; of communion. The matter of the sacraments is plain, earthly: water, bread, wine. But through, with, by, and in them, we are initiated and sustained in the kingdom of heaven. Likewise, the Scriptures: in these earthly texts, the eternal word of God speaks to us.

The sacramental approach to Bible study involves a faithful reception of the *givenness* of the Scriptures in God's good purpose for us. To be sure, all the books of the Bible are in one aspect fully human; that is, they are certainly conditioned in their human particularity. They were written at specific times, places, and circumstances and addressed originally to specific people. Consideration of all these has to go into Biblical scholarship.

The Incarnational Analogy

It is a heresy to deny the full humanity of Jesus (as though he were God merely in human costume).[4] Similarly, it is a serious problem to approach the Bible as though it were some sort of generic document, written in heaven (perhaps on gold tablets), that simply fell straight to earth.

On the other hand, it is also a heresy to view Jesus as not really the one, eternal Son of God incarnate but someone who was only provisionally (and therefore, only artificially) labelled as a divine "son."[5] So, it's a serious problem as well to regard the Scriptures as merely human documents, products of our quest for meaning, that only provisionally (and therefore,

---

4. See the doctrinal affirmations of the Fourth (Chalcedon, 451) and Sixth (Constantinople III, 680) Ecumenical Councils.

5. See those of the First (Nicaea, 325) and Third (Ephesus, 431) Ecumenical Councils.

accidently) might sometimes function as God's word. While one cannot push the analogy too far, the incarnational pattern of understanding the Person of Christ has some highly valuable application to our engagement with Holy Scripture.

The point is that the Scriptures, in all their human particularities, are still a *given* for us: given by God to his people. They are the enduring instrument of his self-disclosure to us. So, not only in an original *then* but also *always*, for us, they are "God-breathed" (2 Tim 3:16 NIV). Thus, we are not to shy away from saying that they do not merely contain or convey but *are* the word of God.

It's About Life, Not Always About What We Think We Want

Needless to say, recognizing this does not eliminate difficulties, challenges, or—sometimes—darkness and discomfort. Nor should we expect that the Bible gives us an easy, ready-to-go script for every ethical quandary we might possibly face. Sometimes what the Bible gives us is a frame in which we must *discern*. And there are times—in good faith—when we might discern differently from one another. (Which is not to say that moral concerns are simply a matter of our own subjective determination or that Scripture never gives us clear moral teaching! Nevertheless, while the Bible is about life, it is not always about clarity and comfort.) For us, hiddenness and disclosure are bound up together in all our possible knowing: most of all, of course, in our knowledge of God.

The Givenness of Scripture

The givenness of Scripture is important to remember when we're dealing with texts we experience as uncongenial, when we really wish something else had been passed down to us. The Grand Inquisitor in Dostoevsky's *Brothers Karamazov* notoriously says to Christ, "We have corrected Thy work, O Lord!"[6] And when we would be tempted—of course, for such very good reasons, and with such noble intentions!—to a similar attitude, it is precisely then that it is most important for us to remember Scripture's givenness.[7]

---

6. Dostoevsky (Garnett), *Brothers Karamazov*, 237.
7. The giver of the Holy Scriptures is God, whose word they are—albeit through

This does not mean that we hunker down in narrow fundamentalisms. Nor does it mean that we are meant to replicate the cultures in which the books of the Bible came to be written. By no means! It also does not it mean that we can forget that the Bible is a library of books containing many different literary genres, written over the course of centuries and at different points in the arc of salvation history.

Christ Is the Center

As Christians, we understand that the center and culmination of the whole Bible—from Genesis through Revelation—is the Person of Jesus Christ. The Bible contains within itself an ongoing, unfolding revelatory narrative that leads to him. In the New Testament, Christ's presence—and his accomplished work—are made explicit for us at last. But that doesn't mean that he wasn't there before—all along. But it's certainly true that his presence is sometimes far more mysterious—and frankly, difficult to discern—in the long journey, before then. When what God gives is mystery, that's what God means for us to have. God makes clear to us what we need to have made clear, not necessarily what we want to be made clear.

Paradoxical Blessings

In all Bible study, we need to remember that we are frequently *meant* to struggle, question, and feel some discomfort. That's part of the gift. It's not always all about clarity, comfort, and affirmation!

"For the word of God is alive and active, sharper than any two-edged sword, to the piercing to division of soul and spirit, of joints and marrow" (Heb 4:12).

---

human instrumentality. The church did not simply "decide" what was (and wasn't) Scripture. Thinking that this was the case is a mistake. The early church considered the writings of the Old and New Testament as the prophetic and apostolic witness by which it itself was constituted. The development of the canon was understood by the church not a matter of its decision but of acknowledgement, recognition, and *reception*.

The Word of God—"who gives life to the dead and calls into existence the things that do not exist" (Rom 4:17)—creates the church, not the other way around. This is why the place of Holy Scripture within the broader life of the church is (and must be) truly unique. Jesus Christ—perfectly, completely, and ultimately—is himself the Word of God (John 1:1-14; see also Col 1:15-17; Heb 1:2-3a). Of all the many venerable elements in the life of the church, it is the Holy Scriptures—*alone*—that share this title with him.

Nor should we expect that the Bible provides us with a path to human uniformity. In it, through it, we can indeed find deepest fellowship—"the peace that passeth all understanding" (Phil 4:7 KJV). But such fellowship (not being a human product but a gift of the Spirit) spans, unexpectedly, across *difference*: personal, cultural, sociopolitical, historical, and—yes— even ecclesiastical difference. For me, this is one of the greatest wonders in the communion of saints.

Receiving, Not Evading

Throughout the whole course of church history, it has been understood that the Bible is the enduring source for our teaching and our worship. It remains the source even when the language it uses, its chosen metaphors, images, and narratives, might be ones we might—with the best of intentions, of course—be tempted to rewrite. My observation is that many churches these days are far too ready to adjust scriptural language to fit present norms of congeniality and simply collapse the distance between then and now. Does staying connected to the source sometimes take us out of our comfort zones? Does it have important practical implications in pastoral care and instruction, as we seek to bridge the gap between the then, in which the books of the Bible came to be written, and our present now—across times, places, and cultures? Yes and yes, of course. But where is it written that either the Bible, or the biblical heritage, always must be inoffensive—never difficult, never risky? Our current affirmation-addicted age needs to remember all this, in particular.

An old wardrobe, stored alone in a drab room, right where we live, just might be our portal to a strange, enduringly new world.[8] So, once again, my conviction is that it is still essential, in faith, for us to cherish the once-for-all givenness of Holy Scripture. And the purpose of this giving was that we might "have life, and have it to the full" (John 10:10 NIV).

Jesus said, "Come to me, all who labor and are heavy laden, and I will give you rest. Take my yoke upon you and learn from me, for I am gentle and lowly in heart, and you will find rest for your souls" (Matt 11:28–29). He *also* said, "Enter by the narrow gate; for the gate is wide and the way is easy that leads to destruction. . . For the gate is narrow and the way is hard, that leads to life" (Matt 7:13, 14).

---

8. Allusions here to Lewis, *Lion, the Witch and the Wardrobe*, and Karl Barth's essay, "The Strange New World Within the Bible," in Barth, *Word of God*, ch. 2.

PREFACE

A Theological Maxim That I Can't Resist Sharing

I will share a classic Reformation theological/hermeneutical maxim with regard to Holy Scripture. Here it is (in its original Latin): that Scripture is [the] *norma normans sed non normata*.[9] That is, Scripture is the "norming norm which is itself not normed." Not normed by anything else, not even

---

9. The maxim, and closely related versions of it, are commonly used in both Lutheran and Reformed circles (but applied somewhat differently). The principle, of course, is a key Reformational commitment from the very beginning. However, tracking down an explicit original citation of the maxim's particular wording itself proved to be something of a challenge. However, thanks to the Reverend Matthew Nelson, I'm able to provide the following: Abraham Calov (Calovius), *Syncretismus Calixtinus* (1653). The concept itself that the maxim came to summarize is well attested in the early church fathers, and during the Reformation from Luther and Calvin, on. The sense in which I apply the concept and use the phrase is aptly expressed in the *Lutheran Formula of Concord*, Epitome and Solid Declaration, Introduction, 1, 2, 7 (1577).

This by no means eliminates the role of historic tradition in the church. Rather, it protects that tradition and its role. The church's great theologians, its normative councils, creeds, and confessions—not to mention the basic shape and content of its liturgy—are to be held in genuinely appreciative respect and given all their due attention. But they are not *norma normans*—"the norm that norms" (Holy Scripture); rather, they are *norma normata*—"the norms that are normed" (normed *by* Holy Scripture).

We aren't to deny the critical role of our ongoing context in—and accountability to—the communion of saints as we engage with Scripture. Such engagement must not be reduced to "private interpretation" (2 Pet 1:20 KJV). We will always read and interpret in one context or another. Again: is there full awareness of—and accountability for—our context, whatever it is? Unacknowledged contexts can be full of pitfalls.

Nevertheless, it will not do simply to appeal to "Scripture *and* tradition." Inevitably, one of these will correct—or "norm"—the other. Theologically and hermeneutically, these two can *never* actually function as coequal governing standards. That they are both valuable, and that in different senses both are needed, is not in question. The question was—and still is: When it comes down to it, which one, ultimately, will "norm" the other? And seeing Scripture just as one element among many *within* tradition is even less workable; in my view, this only leads to downgrading the practical role of Scripture even more. The unique character of the Scriptures is the instrument by which the church itself is sustained under the greater authority of its Lord. These other approaches to the question of governing standard (Scripture *and*, or Scripture *within*, tradition), well-intentioned though they may be, regrettably provide inadequate understandings of the relationship of the Scriptures to the whole of the church's life, and thus leave tradition all-too-open to uncorrectable deteriorations. Hence, the need for clarifications such as the following:

> "Holy Scripture containeth all things necessary to salvation: so that whatsoever is not read therein, nor may be proved thereby, is not to be required of any man, that it should be believed as an article of the Faith, or be thought requisite or necessary to salvation." (Article 6 of "The Articles of Religion," in Book of Common Prayer, 868)

the very best of our concerns and insights. Scripture is the enduring source book of our faith. Only in such a mindset are we opened to the ongoing adventure into which Scripture—as the inexhaustible word of God—draws us. In it, there will always be something new to learn, some new application which before we may not have even suspected. This is true, both personally and across the centuries. But this is a matter of deepening, never disconnection! We have been joined to a great continuum in the "faith that was once for all entrusted to God's holy people" (Jude 3 NIV).

The Incarnate Particular Encompasses the Universal.

When we read the Bible across the wide expanse of very different times and cultures, we do face what's been called the "scandal of particularity." Why did God choose to communicate in the manner in which he did? We might prefer that God had made other choices, that he had broken through to us in different ways: in other words, that the Bible be different than it is. But "must we always be doubting the pastoral wisdom of the Holy Spirit?"[10] Must we always "kick against the goads"? (Acts 26:14).

In the providence of God, the incarnate particular encompasses the universal. This is most fully true in the incarnation of Jesus Christ. His earthly time holds *all* times—his earthly place, then, all places and all circumstances. In the dusty, sweat-stained face of our incarnate Lord, we behold—as fully as we can—the cosmic Christ. In him, nothing has been held back. We must not look for some revelation behind the revelation.

In analogous ways, this concept also applies to the word of God written: the incarnate particular encompasses the universal.

Reading as Encounter

C. S. Lewis, in one of his last books, *An Experiment in Criticism*, wrote about engaging with works of art. What he said there goes with human communication, in general, and most of all, with Holy Scripture.

> The first demand any work of art makes upon us is surrender. Look. Listen. Receive. Get yourself out of the way. (There is no good asking first whether the work before you deserves such a

---

10. For the citation for this apt question, see the introduction to this volume.

surrender, for until you have surrendered you cannot possibly find out.)[11]

This is important advice, because—unless the impulse is somehow held in check—we are all too likely to jump to reactivities and so miss out on what a real encounter might have had in store. The time comes for our active response, of course, but the initial surrender Lewis speaks of is essential if we want to get to the room with a view (as opposed to hunkering down in a hall of mirrors).

We must allow the books of Scripture—in all their variety, all their layers of meaning, in all their challenges, their paradoxes, and their clarities—to speak to us on their own terms. The *whole* Bible—from Genesis through Revelation—is, for us, the Word of Jesus Christ, who is himself the one eternal Word of God. Sometimes in the Bible, Christ seems more hidden; sometimes, to be sure, he is more explicitly disclosed. But in all of it, when and as he wills, he gives himself to us. And he can do so, both when we are eagerly seeking him, and also—thanks be!—when we are determined to be on the run from him.

Reading Whole Books of the Bible

There is an irreplaceable value in reading the various books of the Bible as the complete texts that they are—and to do so in a sufficiently focused time frame, so that one gets the full impact of each book as a literary whole. However, for a number of practical reasons, I don't usually recommend trying to go through the Bible simply in its canonical order, straight through, all the way from Genesis to Revelation. Instead, there are a number of practical reading plans which take one through all of Holy Scripture, which combine reading from different books at the same time, and which include—or interlace—both Old and New Testament. Robert Murray McCheyne's *Daily Bread* schedule is a classic, with very much to be said for it—although for most people, I often suggest that it be stretched out to a two-year plan. Even here, going through books at only a chapter a day can sometimes thin out the full effect that a more concentrated reading of a whole book provides.

Of course, there's plenty of occasion for highly detailed study of particular passages too. But if the great bulk of all our reading were just picking

---

11. Lewis, *Experiment in Criticism*, 19.

Preface

out isolated paragraphs here and there, we'd obviously be missing out on most of what reading has to offer us. So, too, with Scripture.

Reading in Context of the Whole: The Example of the Gospels

Our lectionary (and any possible lectionary based on the church year) disguises the place of the Gospels' passion narratives within their respective wholes. For the most part, the lectionaries corral these narratives into one week of the year. One of fifty-two.

Yet note the portions in the four Gospels, from the Entrance into Jerusalem ("Palm Sunday") on. In both Mark and John, this is over 40 per cent; in Luke, over 25. In Matthew, it's a full third. Our church year, and lectionaries, are both good ideas for many good reasons. But we need to take care not to forget broader contexts—which is all too easy to do if we're paying most of our attention just to week-by-week lectionary snippets. The Gospels are not collections of isolated sayings and events. They are, rather, highly integrated narratives in which the parts must be considered in light of the whole. If we read and study—and teach—the Gospels as the literary wholes that they are, it's colossally evident, from their very opening pages, that they all display a relentless, increasing focus forward, to the cross.

When we "hear . . . read, mark, learn, and inwardly digest"[12] the Gospels as a whole, we will be inoculated against the unsustainable notion that Jesus was mostly about moral exhortation; that the Gospel narratives are simply about someone "who came to show us how to live"; that our core problem, therefore, was lack of information.

Even though our week-by-week lectionary Gospel readings, considered by themselves, might sometimes be treated merely as episodes of moral exhortation, when they are read in their full contexts, these passages are rightly seen as what they are: fully integrated elements in a narrative arc of cosmic redemption—a narrative that culminates at Golgotha and the empty tomb. What we needed was not simply more information but an apocalyptic intervention to set us free from the captivating powers of sin and death.[13]

---

12. *Book of Common Prayer*, 184, 236.

13. For a highly recommended introduction to and exposition of this theme, see Rutledge, *Crucifixion*, 348–94.

When read as the literary wholes that they are, it is utterly clear that Matthew, Mark, Luke, and John, each in their own way, and in their own words, also witness to a Jesus who, in God's saving purpose, is "the Lamb slain from the foundation of the world" τοῦ ἀρνίου τοῦ ἐσφαγμένου ἀπὸ καταβολῆς κόσμου (Rev 13:8 KJV; also 1 Pet 1:18–20). They, too, witness to a Christ through whom "God was pleased . . . to reconcile to himself all things, whether on earth or in heaven, by making peace through the blood of his cross" (Col 1:19, 20).

The Surpassing Worth

Reading the Bible is not an unceasing mountaintop experience, both because of what the Bible is and also what we are. Not every chapter of Scripture is the summit of Everest. (Although I've often said that if I had to say which chapter is that summit, for me, it would be the eighth chapter of Paul's Letter to the Romans). Scripture is a vast landscape that takes us to valleys and dry places, too. And we don't live in a non-stop spiritual honeymoon, either. What matters is keeping to the long journey into which God has led us. That doesn't just happen by following our own paths of least resistance. Leading a Scripture-soaked life requires commitment and discipline. There are choices to be made. I have been blessed to be able to say that the choices involved in getting to such a life are infinitely worth it. But, as always—thanks be—above, beneath, and prior to all our own possible choosing is God's choice, God's summons: in Christ, and by the power of the Holy Spirit.

> "Lord, to whom shall we go? You have the words of eternal life." (John 6:68)

Introduction

THE FOLLOWING IS A selection from my preaching from 1996 through 2024: twenty-eight sermons, the first fourteen of these from my reception into the Episcopal Church up through my retirement in 2019, and the last fourteen, from after retirement. The heavier weight on my more recent preaching stems both from a desire to convey "where I am," at present, as well as more fully addressing what I see as the current spiritual condition and needs of the church.

"Which Adam?" through "The Table with the Open Space" were delivered at Church of the Good Shepherd, Ogden, Utah, and "But We See Jesus" through "Grant Us, O Lord, to Trust in You with All Our Hearts" at Church of the Holy Spirit, Orleans, Massachusetts. (At both of these congregations I was honored to serve as rector.)

Some of these sermons were delivered from full scripts. However, a substantial number of them were either given from spare notes, or without written notes at all, and later transcribed. But even these latter were not extemporaneous. Rather, they were the product of full planning and preparation.

I've sought to keep a modest editorial touch. Over the years that these sermons encompass, I certainly developed. I was not the same in 1996 as I was in 2024—indeed, I should hope not! However, to give a better sense of the greater whole of my preaching ministry, to fill in at least a few blanks, to avoid some repetition, and to make some things a little clearer—I have made a number of adjustments and adaptations to the texts as they are here. (This, in distinction to the *ipsissima verba* of these sermons on their original dates of delivery.) But I have resisted the temptation of trying to present myself as saying "then" what I would say now.

I have not provided any commentary on the pastoral contexts of these sermons, preferring instead to let them speak for themselves. In looking

Introduction

this collection over, I find a fair number of them have autobiographical illustrations; a notably much greater percentage than was usual in my sermons. Yet for other reasons, these seemed to be the right ones to include in this collection, and perhaps such personal references are more apt in a summarizing anthology as well.

Preaching is—or ought to be—intensely situational. Certainly, it is part of the preacher's role to strengthen further what is already strong. But that role must also include addressing the tendencies to all that which may be lacking or unhealthy. There can be much discernment, and much pondering, of the issues of integrity, in finding the balance. Nevertheless, to use nautical imagery: sooner or later, faithful preachers will inevitably find themselves in situations in which they will need to provide some spiritual "live ballast" to counteract an unhelpful—or even dangerous—heeling over. The degree of this live ballast varies with the needs of the time. And sometimes it's a matter not of heeling (in response to exterior circumstances) but listing (from the interior condition of the vessel itself).

While preachers do need to help situate their people nourishingly within their particular Christian tradition, neither will it do simply to provide what amounts to a diet of spiritual flattery. The habit of constant (or near-constant) institutional self-referentiality, even in the most sacred precincts, is only a hair's breadth away from out-and-out idolatry.[1]

---

[1]. Our Lord said, "I will build my church, and the powers of death shall not prevail against it" (Matt 16:18). I doubt that he had any illusions at all about who and what he would be working with, but on balance, he clearly thought it a good idea and a necessary part of the plan. The church is (and is to be) "the pillar and bulwark of the truth" (1 Tim 3:15). Both the Apostles' and Nicene Creeds include profession of belief *in* the church itself.

So for Christians there is (or should be) an appropriate zeal for—and necessary loyalty to—the church. And yet we—even (perhaps sometimes *especially*) in pious contexts—are all too likely to make things "all about us." Some words of Karl Barth—in their usual distinctive way—might serve well as a salutary corrective when tempted to any form of ecclesiastical narcissism:

> The activity of the community is related to the Gospel only in so far as it is no more than a crater formed by the explosion of a shell and seeks to be no more than a void in which the Gospel reveals itself. The people of Christ, His community, know that no sacred word or work or thing exists in its own right: they know only those words and works and things which by their negation are sign-posts to the Holy One. If anything Christian(!) be unrelated to the Gospel, it is a human by-product, a dangerous religious survival, a regrettable misunderstanding. For in this case content would be substituted for a void, convex for concave, positive for negative, and the characteristic marks of Christianity would be possession and

INTRODUCTION

On the other hand, being contrary just for its own sake is another seriously unhealthy habit. It can become very self-indulgent. The call to preach exists within specific church contexts. When a church sets someone apart to do so, it does more than provide the preacher with some sort of personal stage. Preaching with integrity requires a basic rootedness in, and accountability to, the ordaining church and its core doctrine and practice. This includes a solid awareness of—and positive engagement with—the classic theological resources of one's own particular church tradition; and hopefully, too, some good experience with other key resources elsewhere within historic Christianity.

This does not rule out all individual perspectives or concerns that preachers may bring to their work; nor does it rule out offering ballast—or challenge—to the church when such are needed. Far from it. But if preaching within a basic ecclesiastical integrity is not (or is no longer) possible within one's own setting, one should not do so.

To be sure, sorting this out can be a demanding discernment; requiring much honesty, self-awareness, good counsel, and—most of all—recourse to the Grace of God.

Readers should not look to this present collection for any sort of comprehensive systematic theology, nor even complete coverage of any one element of such a theology, but rather themes that I thought were especially needful. And while I hope that this present anthology is representative in a broader sense, it certainly is not exhaustive. The omission, here, of any particular topic does not mean that I didn't think it important—or that I didn't preach on it, elsewhere.

---

self-sufficiency rather than deprivation and hope." (Barth, *Epistle to the Romans*, 36)

We being what we are, the religious enterprise can all too easily devolve into a massive evasion of its stated goal. There's a telling bit of dialogue in Bernard Malamud's masterful short story "The Magic Barrel," in which the protagonist—recently having completed his theological studies and anticipating ordination—comes to a disruptive realization:

"When . . . did you become enamored of God?" . . .

". . . I came to God not because I loved Him but because I did not." (Malamud, *Complete Stories*, 142)

But such uncomfortable awarenesses need not be a counsel of despair. They could be early breathings of the regenerating Spirit. "Where sin increased, grace abounded all the more" (Rom 5:20).

INTRODUCTION

Likewise, those wondering why I seem not to have addressed contemporary issues as much as many of my colleagues, I would mention the following: first, that I did so more often than this set of sermons might convey, and second, when I did, I often chose to do so in a rather different manner than many of my fellow preachers.

It seemed to be a rare disposition, but I strenuously sought to avoid tipping my hand—even subtly—in terms of social-political affiliations.

Preaching is not "my turn to talk," but commissioned speech on behalf of an Other. The homiletic addressing of present-day concerns—surely sometimes necessary—has to be governed under that rubric and also must be attuned to the preacher's sense of the congregation's actual spiritual needs as it grapples with the issues of the day. (And I was quite sure that my people's most pressing spiritual need was certainly not that they agreed with my own particular assessments of this or that presenting issue of the time.)

Preachers cannot possibly know the full "results" of their preaching. (That's not really their business.) But to the extent that I could have a sense of it, my sermons "worked," most often, incrementally. The difference they made was usually a matter of cumulative effect over the course of an extended ministry. I often called it "timed release."

In terms of "technique," my sermons were often idiosyncratic. This may be for a number of reasons. One of these might be my early training in music, from childhood through my undergraduate major in college. Musical forms likely informed the structures of my sermons. Another might be the years that I heard rabbinic preaching—during the substantial period in which I was away from church but attending synagogue services on a somewhat regular basis (a part of my spiritual formation for which I remain profoundly grateful). This exposed me to a different approach to the homiletic enterprise, as did my decades in the Eastern Orthodox Church, as member and as priest. Also to be kept in mind is that my most characteristic mode of delivery was without script (albeit fully prepared). And lastly, my approach to preaching—and life, in general—seems to be highly intuitional. So, in terms of style and form (as opposed to content), I'd be concerned if my preaching were to be taken as some sort of generic model. What worked for me, and—I hope—my congregations, likely would not work as an all-purpose sermonic exemplar.

Sermons are an *oral* form of communication. Although they certainly contain instruction, they aren't to be essays read aloud. As I've prepared

Introduction

this collection, I have not erased their oral character, nor—for better or worse—have I eliminated my own speaking style. This seemed all the more fitting given the fact that many of these sermons were delivered without script.

One matter deserves additional comment: when I spoke of God, I kept to the norms found in Holy Scripture, including the use of the masculine personal pronoun. I was well aware of the issues around this. But for me, and for various reasons both theological and linguistic, the argument against keeping to the biblical and historic usages has been "weighed in the balances, and . . . found wanting" (Dan 5:27, KJV).

It is appropriate to name what and who have been especially important in my own theological and pastoral formation, specifically as it related to my ministry as a preacher. But nothing—or no one—I will mention here is responsible for my many shortcomings (homiletic or otherwise). Just that for any good that may have been found in my preaching (or may be found by those who will read these sermons), I owe incalculable debts of gratitude.

Of course, such acknowledgements must begin with—and continue to be founded in—the Holy Scriptures of the Old and New Testament. The word of God is the indispensable fount for any preaching worthy of the name. For more on what I have to say about this, please see the preface in this volume, "Holy Scripture: What It Is and How to Read it." In that essay, I make explicit my approach to the Bible, which in the sermons which follow, was implicit.

My formal pastoral education comes out of two distinct Christian theological groundings: first, Eastern Orthodox, and then, Reformed. An interesting combination to be sure, with some tensions, but also—for me—some remarkable intersections. Although my broader trajectory over the years certainly was decisively toward the Reformed, appropriated within an historic Anglican context,[2] in important respects I have not left behind the gifts to be found in the witness of the Eastern Church—nor do I have any intention of doing so.

---

2. Initially "Anglican" was unquestionably a subset (albeit a distinctive one) within the Reformed movement, as any attentive reading of the *Book of Common Prayer*, the *Books of Homilies*, the *Articles of Religion*, the works of Richard Hooker, the sermons of John Donne, and indeed—with the exception of Archbishop Laud—just about anything else from the Church of England in the sixteenth and early seventeenth centuries will make abundantly clear.

Introduction

Preachers would do very well to be steeped in the church fathers: Irenaeus of Lyons and Athanasius of Alexandria; Basil the Great, Gregory of Nazianzus, and Gregory of Nyssa (these three—especially and enduringly formulative for me—known collectively as the Cappadocian Fathers); John Chrysostom, of course; and Augustine of Hippo (whom in recent years I have come to appreciate more and more). A thorough acquaintance with the doctrinal formulations of the seven Ecumenical Councils is very highly recommended (if not urged) as well.

Additional theologians, writers, and preachers whom I need to mention include Isaac the Syrian, Julian of Norwich, John Calvin, Richard Hooker (cited by many but read by few), as well as George Herbert, John Donne (both as a poet and a preacher), John Bunyan, and Gerard Manley Hopkins.

Coming closer to our own time brings Karl Barth (in particular), Georges Florovsky, Martyn Lloyd-Jones, Michael Ramsey, Dallas Willard, and Eugene Peterson into my personal mix. In the literary realm, Fyodor Dostoevsky, Joseph Conrad, Flannery O'Connor, and J. R. R. Tolkien must not be omitted from mention, either. And bridging the literary and the theological is C. S. Lewis, whose critical importance for me, over many years, is impossible to overestimate.

That's quite a disparate lineup, I know. Perhaps in earthly terms they might be rather surprised to find themselves associated with one another—and with me—but there they are.

Music has meant more to me than I can say and certainly has had a critical role to play in my formation as a human being, as a Christian, and also as a preacher. Utterly preeminent among those to name here, of course, is J. S. Bach. Nothing I could say would be remotely adequate, and even if I tried, "time would fail me to tell" (Heb 11:32). Also to mention would certainly be the hymns of Martin Luther and those of the great Lutheran hymn writers who followed him: among these, "Christ Jesus Lay in Death's Strong Bands,"[3] "A Mighty Fortress,"[4] "Sleepers, Wake!,"[5] "How Bright Ap-

---

3. Martin Luther, "Christ lag in Todesbanden," in *Hymnal 1982*, #186.

4. Martin Luther, "Ein feste Burg," in *Hymnal 1982*, #688.

5. Philipp Nicolai, "Wachet auf," in *Hymnal 1982*, #61. This in particular, through a listening to Bach's Cantata based on this hymn on a summer morning before I started college (1972), was the instrument of an early unsettling awareness that maybe I wasn't nearly as "through with Christianity" as I had thought. That summer morning listening session combined aesthetic delight (which I expected) with an undeniable sense of spiritual connection (which I certainly did not expect).

INTRODUCTION

pears the Morning Star,"[6] and "Ah, Holy Jesus"[7] (this last, in my estimation, the greatest single Holy Week hymn from any Christian tradition, bar none). Neither could I omit Charles Wesley, Anglican, whose hymns are an enduring treasury of faith and whose "And Can It Be,"[8] if any one hymn could come close to "saying it all," would be it. These and such as these are among the load-bearing beams in the structure of my faith.

Two whom I've been blessed to know here and now, in the flesh, who made decisive contributions to my development as a preacher, are the late James Doyle, teacher, mentor, colleague, and much missed dear friend, and Fleming Rutledge, a colleague who has fortified the best in me, from whom I have learned much, and whose friendship has been a cherished blessing.

For the challenging question that I pose in the preface, "Must we always be doubting the pastoral wisdom of the Holy Spirit?," full credit must be given to Sean McDonough (Professor of New Testament, Gordon-Conwell Theological Seminary, South Hamilton, Massachusetts), from whom I first heard it. Special thanks are also due to my good friend and scholarly colleague Samuel Micah Hunter for his proofreading this anthology and providing a generous number of helpful comments.

Lastly, I owe uttermost thanks to my dear wife, Lori, my life companion and partner, for so many things—more than I could possibly here enumerate. But relevant to this present endeavor I should mention that she transcribed many of these sermons from their original audio recordings, as well as offering keen observations on the first drafts of their written versions.

Reviewing this collection, I certainly have a keen sense of both inadequacy and maybe even presumption, but also—by God's grace—of love. And may his mercy "heal all that which is infirm, and complete all that which is lacking" (Prayer of Ordination, Byzantine Rite).[9]

Within the sermons (excepting the last one, "Receive the Kingdom of God as a Little Child") unless otherwise indicated, all Scripture citations are taken from the New Revised Standard Version, as this was the translation then in standard use in the Episcopal Church. Citations in the final sermon, unless otherwise indicated, are taken from the Authorized King James Version. (My use of it, there, was an affectionate allusion to a pivotal

---

6. Philipp Nicolai, "Wie schön leuchtet," in *Hymnal 1982*, #497.
7. Johann Heerman, "Herzliebster Jesu," in *Hymnal 1982*, #158.
8. Regrettably not included in *Hymnal 1982*.
9. See Hapgood, *Service Book*, 312, 316, 329.

Introduction

encounter of mine with Scripture, in that translation, which I recounted in that same sermon.) All other citations (again, unless otherwise identified) are from the Revised Standard Version.

References to *The Book of Common Prayer* are that of the Episcopal Church (1979).

"From the East Gate"
Saint Christopher's Church, Oak Park, Illinois

Year A, Proper 14: Jonah 2:1–9; Matt 14:22–33
Sunday, August 8, 1996
First Sermon in the Episcopal Church

"You cast me into the deep, into the heart of the seas, and the flood surrounded me; all your waves and billows passed over me. Then I said, 'I am driven away from your sight; how shall I look again upon your holy temple?'" (Jonah 2:3–4)

THIS SUNDAY'S OLD TESTAMENT lection is Jonah's voice from the heart of the storm: a prayer made from a series of psalm verses. Oddly enough, his prayer is one of *thanksgiving*, proceeding from lament to praise for deliverance—even while still entombed in the belly of the great fish.

The French aviator Antoine de Saint Exupéry, beginning one of his essays in *Wind, Sand and Stars*, writes:

> When Joseph Conrad described a typhoon he said very little about towering waves, or darkness, or the whistling of the wind in the shrouds. He knew better. Instead, he took his readers down into the hold of the vessel, packed with emigrant[s], . . . where the rolling and pitching of the ship had ripped up and scattered their bags and bundles, burst open their boxes, and flung their belongings into a crazy heap. Family treasures painfully collected in a lifetime of poverty, pitiful mementoes so alike that nobody but their owners could have told them apart, had lost their identity and lapsed into chaos, into anonymity . . . It was this human drama that Conrad described when he painted a typhoon.[1]

---

1. From "The Elements," in Saint-Exupéry, *Wind, Sand and Stars*, 48.

From the East Gate

In biblical imagery, waters, particularly stormy waters, evoke destruction, return to chaos—the very opposite of human security within creation. Watery tumult threatens our sense of place, proportion, and stability. That these are tremendously important to us often only becomes evident in their absence—and in their absence, our own identity is perhaps no longer clear. Hence, we are creatures with a great hunger for predictability and control. We prefer, at least for much of the time, a stable earth.

I suppose that different cultures and individuals have their own distinct images for threat to the comfortable order of things. I'm reminded of my family's recent trip out to Glacier National Park. For much of the eastern side of the Rockies, the mountains emerge fairly suddenly from the plains. We had never been to Glacier. There are two principal gates. Coming from our direction, the west side entrance went through the lower pass and skirted under the park. The east entrance (the direction from which we were coming) would take us on the scenic route through the heart of matters. Let's just say that for a couple of hours before we arrived at the mountains, we had a cordial yet nevertheless "frank and open exchange of views" about which entrance to the park we would take. I got my way. The east gate it would be. I have to tell you, though, that fairly soon into the enterprise, I was glad that I wasn't driving. More significantly, everyone else in the car was glad that I wasn't driving. Whoever had given the road its name, "Going to the Sun Highway," was much more of a literalist than I would have previously expected. The experience was tremendously enjoyable. However, I have to confess that to appreciate the journey over the top properly, at a few critical points I found that I had to take my glasses off. The passage was beautiful—indeed, extraordinarily so. I had seen mountains but never anything like these. There was almost too much beauty to bear, too much expanse of height and depth to comprehend, such as to swamp the imagination—to overcome the usual sense of human place and proportion. It is difficult to know whether such an experience is more intimidating on land or at sea. I *was* reminded that getting what one thinks is one's way can be a risky thing.

> Then Jonah prayed to the Lord his God from [his entombment in] the belly of the fish, saying, "I called to the Lord out of my distress, and he answered me; out of the belly of Sheol I cried, and you heard my voice." (2:1–2)

God speaks from the midst of the storm. Perhaps we ought to be somewhat more critical of our hunger for security. At least sometimes, it is necessary that militant assurance pass away before the divine word may be heard once again in power and clarity. God remains God. Does not our Lord's life and ministry have something to say about our pursuit of control? I think, as well, that Saint Paul's contrast of grace with law has a distinct bearing on human insistence on a constant religious assurance. It is a very human inclination to fill in the blanks, to establish for ourselves a too-impervious and constant knowing. However, this is an inclination which needs to be evaluated with great care. The way of grace is a way of openness. Openness leads us to accept the course of our journey of faith, including times of disruption—accepting also times of the absence and silence of God. Better the absence of the true God than the presence of an idol; better God's silence than words we put in God's mouth. Finally, better the providential storm than an artificial yet merely human peace.

Yet the way of grace is also a way of centeredness. In faith we remain centered on the One who is our "true loyalty," the One in whom is life, the light of all people (Jonah 2:8; John 1:3b).

> "You brought up my life from the pit, O Lord my God. As my life was ebbing away, I remembered the Lord; and my prayer came to you, into your holy temple." (2:6–7)

From the midst of the storm, Christ came to the disciples and bid Peter to step out upon the waters. Times come when our Lord, indeed, calls us to step out from the world that has been. Perhaps it may be that the markers of our life, the components of what we have known as our identity, will lay jumbled about for a while. However, for Christians, if such a movement is faithful, it is a Christ-ward movement, centered on him and in a living continuity with his body, the church.

It seems clear that in faith, persons and communities are called to be *both* open and centered. Admittedly, this is a difficult balance to maintain. Working out this challenging balance is a key part of our spiritual growth. An uncentered "openness" is more likely to be adrift than open. That which is distracted and adrift is all too likely to sink. In the Person of our incarnate Lord, crucified and risen for us, "the grace of God has dawned upon the world with healing for all" (Titus 2:11 REB). Lest we sink into the tumult, we are enjoined to fix our spiritual gaze on the One who is "the pioneer and perfecter of our faith" (Heb 12:2).

However, it might also be questioned if an unopen, supposed "centeredness" is really centered on Christ in the first place. We are called to step out to our Lord in faith—out of comfortable securities we have known—to a radical newness: a way of ongoing freedom and service. "I came that [you] may have life, and have it abundantly" (John 10:10). Is it consistent with this new life that we would again be so very consumed with the drawing of human boundaries and the establishment of human control?

As God remains God, so also grace remains grace: all-encompassing yet ungraspable, inexhaustible. We are led to accept risk: the self-displacing storm, the majesty and beauty which seem too much for our separateness to bear. It may be, after all, that it is precisely in these that we will hear the voice of Christ bidding us draw near. The freedom of the gospel enables us to receive what is brought to us in both centered and open hearts. Instead of destruction, what we meet in gracious risk is new creation. Our identity, our place, and our entire notion of security are redefined. Mere acceptance isn't quite a fully adequate response. Rather, we are led in spirit to what must seem now an often enigmatic yet still transcendent thankfulness. In grace, we are led to eucharistic life.

> "The deep surrounded me . . . at the roots of the mountains. But I, with the voice of thanksgiving, will sacrifice to you." (2:5, 9)

"Which Adam?"

The Church of the Good Shepherd, Ogden, Utah

Year A, Proper 7. Rom 5:15–19
Sunday, June 19, 2005

WE FIND OURSELVES INVOLVED in a larger story not of our own choosing. Perhaps sometimes it feels as though we are characters in a novel trying to figure out the plot (and our place in it) as the book goes along. An essential part of all authentic human "figuring out" is conversation—and sometimes debate—with others. So, it is no coincidence that conversation and debate are the Jewish, and therefore the biblical, way of doing theology.

Paul the apostle, in spite of the key distinctives that set him apart from his background, remains, in his methodology, classically Jewish—truly rabbinic. So, we can never understand Paul's writings unless we appreciate their conversational character. Getting a sense of who the conversation partners are is indispensable to a productive reading of the epistles.

Some of these were those of Paul's own day: supporters, opponents, and—of course—those with whom he wished to share the gospel. Others were voices of earlier times—most importantly, the ancient Hebrew Scriptures. And, by Spirit-intended extension, *we* become partners. We, too, are drawn into the circle.

Surely, it is not always clear what we are to do with this. Paul's style can be described—politely—as dense. He loves long sentences in which, as readers, we have to play challenging rounds of "Let's Find the Main Verb." And frankly, a number of us, at least some of the time, find his content off-putting. Yet, most Sundays of the year, in the second Scripture lesson, we are given Paul to hear. His writings make up both a substantial part, and the earliest part, of our New Testament. Across centuries, often cited by differing sides in heated theological debates, we find him close to the action throughout the history of Christianity. Therefore, wrestling with Paul is to be a part of the deal for us. I personally wouldn't have it otherwise.

So, here we are. Before we go on, I suggest that we hear today's passage again, from another version. Not to discount the New Revised Standard Version that we (and most Episcopal congregations) use on a regular basis. But it's good to keep well in mind that the Scriptures we read and hear are *translations*. Language being what it is, it simply is not possible to have one perfect translation of a text from one tongue to another. Sparing the endeavor of learning biblical languages (Hebrew and Greek), most of us still have easy access to reading passages from more than one rendering. This gives additional lines of sight into a text—often quite a valuable thing. A version that I check often, especially for Paul, is the Revised English Bible.

So, from this version, here is today's New Testament lesson, from Romans:

> "But God's act of grace is out of all proportion to Adam's wrongdoing. For if the wrongdoing of that one man brought death upon so many, its effect is vastly exceeded by the grace of God and the gift of the one man, Jesus Christ. And again, the gift of God is not to be compared in its effect with that one man's sin; for the judicial action, following on the one offense, resulted in a verdict of condemnation, but the act of grace, following on so many misdeeds, resulted in a verdict of acquittal. If by the wrongdoing of one man, death established its reign through that one man, much more shall those who in far greater measure receive grace and the gift of righteousness live and reign through the one man, Jesus Christ. It follows, then, that as the result of one misdeed was condemnation for all people, so the result of one righteous act is acquittal and life for all. For through the disobedience of one man many were made sinners, so through the obedience of one man many will be made righteous." (5:15–19)

Paul is continuing his conversational engagement with the book of Genesis. Just a bit ago, he was discussing the figure of Abraham. Now, he is looking at Christ in relation to Adam.

To get a fuller sense of what Paul is talking about here, it is worth taking more of a look at the Adam story that we find in Genesis. Keep in mind that in Hebrew, "Adam" means "the human."

"In the beginning God created" (Gen 1:1 RSV). And in the story of the process of his creation, we read, repeatedly, "And God saw that it was good" (Gen 1:4, 10, 12, 18, 21, 25). But now, depending on one's perspective at any given point of time, we can say that our life—our world—is either "charged with the grandeur of God" (to recall Gerard Manley Hopkins's great poem)[1] or haunted by that same presence. We can respond to that divine grandeur in very different ways: either as a haunting against which we try to anesthetize ourselves—or as an enlivening (albeit risky) glory to be embraced.

Somehow, we find the impulses for both these responses in us. The Adam story tells us that of our creation in the divine "image and likeness." We must therefore affirm that primal goodness. "And indeed, it was very good" (1:31). Nevertheless, we find a transcendent longing in ourselves as well—to which creation indeed points but which creation itself can never satisfy. For such longing, we are called to look to the One who is the source of all good.

However, as Genesis also tells us, all did not go well in the garden. We read there of a primal crisis; a terrible fall. So now, once our various distractions and anesthetics get taken from us, we find—inescapably—in these selves of ours, an undeniable sense of disruption, of deep loss, of estrangement—cut off, somehow, from Eden. We discover that we are working with means utterly insufficient to reach our best and truest desire. And our predicament cannot be reduced to something "out there." The problem is also *interior*. Along with a remembrance of primal divine goodness, we find ourselves struggling with our present defining identity—our "Adam-ness." We find, in the stuff of what we are, that we are working with a nature that has become—always, to some extent—betraying of ourselves and others.

This narrative is the counterpoint to what we hear from Paul today. Over against this, Paul affirms that in Jesus, God has written a new story. In Christ, a new source of our identity is set forth. In another, closely related passage, Paul writes, "Thus it is written, 'The first man, Adam, became a living being'; the *last* Adam became a life-giving spirit" (1 Cor 15:45). But what script—or, rather whose script—will we live out? In which Adam will our defining humanity be found?

In the here and now, the two Adams sum up, for us, two ways of being—each appropriated rather differently. The first, that of the primal human, almost isn't appropriated at all; it just "is." It's our inherited reality: the life that plays out on its own accord and is lived in accord with our nature as we now find it. The source image is parental. We're speaking here of what Paul would call the "fleshly." This is the world defined by what we possess,

---

1. Hopkins, *Poems and Prose*, 27.

what we earn, and by what we think we can control. Its key words would be "on our own." But because we're finite and because we're sinners, such a path ultimately must lead to a dead end.

The way of the Second Adam is renewed creation. It's not a matter of the life that "just is" but of *adoption*, appropriated by faith, through the One who became our brother. This is the world defined by the gift of God—and *its* key word is "grace." We live now out of the gift and in the sharing of gift. Because God is who God is, the journey of grace is inexhaustible. This "road goes ever on and on."[2]

So, thanks be, in Christ, it's not a matter of getting what we have coming. God has something much better in mind for us. Each day, God summons us to readdress the questions: Which story is becoming *our* story? Will we live on our own or by the gift? In which Adam will we find ourselves? Whose people will we be?

Each time we gather as the church for Eucharist, the gracious invitation is set forth: "The gifts of God for the *People of God*."[3] The Episcopal Church's practice concerning who it admits to the sacrament of holy communion has significantly evolved in the last generation. That evolution is continuing.[4]

Yet "inclusion" becomes meaningless if we have no sense of *what* it is we are welcoming people to. Anglicans have always conveyed much by the language we use in worship. So it is more than appropriate that we be mindful of what we say at our eucharistic invitation. Something that only conveys "you can get bread and wine up this-a-way" is utterly inadequate.

---

2. Tolkien, *Fellowship of the Ring*, 35.

3. *Book of Common Prayer*, 364.

4. When I was a child it was still the practice that one needed to be confirmed in order to receive holy communion in the Episcopal Church. In the intervening years until my return, several steps were taken toward "open communion," leading to offering it to all baptized persons (baptized in any church), the theoretical norm during the time of my ministry in it. The canonical stipulation stated, "No unbaptized person shall be eligible to receive Holy Communion in this church" (1.17.7, *Constitution and Canons*), a norm fully consistent with all historic Christian practice. Nevertheless, that formal stipulation was commonly contradicted, explicitly and publicly, in many Episcopal parishes, which often extended eucharistic invitations irrespective of baptism, faith in Christ, or even belief in God. Whatever good intentions might lie behind invitations such as this, one has to ask what has become of the sense of numinous risk—the *mysterium tremendum*—in relation to receiving the Eucharist. This sense goes right along with—and indeed, is part of—the gratitude, wonder, and joy. (See Otto, *Idea of the Holy*, not to mention, of course, 1 Cor 11:27–29.)

It isn't being true to ourselves, others, or what is going on; it would be both dishonest and unfaithful.

For *all* of us who are here, to get up from our places and draw near to the altar when the celebrant says, "The gifts of God for the people of God" is a remarkable thing to do—numinous, maybe even risky. After all, we're taking our life in our hands!

When we draw near to receive, we are acknowledging that we have been claimed in a Christly claiming; we are acknowledging our profoundest need for the life of the One who died for us. "The Body of Christ, the Bread of Heaven; the Blood of Christ, the Cup of Salvation."[5]

We're living by the gift now. It's no more "our own" process. We can trust the God who has brought us this far to lead us on the journey.

But this we do affirm: that in this Christ-life, so generously given, we are borne into the adventure of new creation. We're in it together now. In ways almost always mundane and everyday, often fairly unremarkable, we find that neither we, nor our stories, nor anything else, can ever be quite the same.

> Where sin increased, grace abounded all the more. (Rom 5:20)

---

5. *Book of Common Prayer*, 365.

"The Binding of God?"

The Great Vigil of Easter: Gen 22:1–18

April 7, 2007

Alleluia! Christ is risen!

This is the night unlike all other nights; this is the night brighter than the day!

Even though it is only gradually coming back into prominence in our worship schedules, it is this, the Great Vigil, which is the quintessential Easter service. If we had to pick one worship event in the whole liturgical year that comes closest to "saying it all," this would be it. Tonight we celebrate our transit—our Passover—from darkness to light. It might be asked, though: since the resurrection of Jesus Christ is our present, foundational reality as a people of faith, why bother with reenacting, in our devotion, this transit? Are we not already, in Christ, children of light? Well—yes, we are; we are, indeed. And yet, this present existence of ours is still, for a time, intersecting with darkness, isn't it?

Yes, in the risen Christ, our decisive transfer is already accomplished. But we live, now, in between: still emerging from where and what we have been and continuing, also, to enter into that which has been accomplished—that which is held for us in gracious trust.

Awareness of the striking contrast between light and dark is a key part of what gives this particular service its needful power.

> "Do you not know that all of us who have been baptized into Christ Jesus were baptized into his death?" (Rom 6:3)

Perhaps, in some other mode of being yet to come for us, the key thing to know will be "Christ is glorified!" Now, though, that key thing is that the crucified Christ is risen: risen from death.

"The Binding of God?"

In the opinion of many, the greatest Easter hymn of the Reformation (and, indeed, one of the greatest in all Christian hymnody) is *Christ lag in Todesbanden*, written by Martin Luther, translated in our hymnal as "Christ Jesus lay in death's strong bands." It expresses, magnificently, our essential affirmation of faith. Later in this service, we'll sing it as our offertory hymn. I'd like to share a bit of it with you now, ahead of time:

> Christ Jesus lay in death's strong bands for our offenses given . . .
> It was a strange and dreadful strife when life and death contended;
> The victory remained with life, the reign of death was ended . . .
> Then let us feast this holy day on the true bread of heaven . . .
> He is our meat and drink indeed; faith lives upon no other!
> Alleluia![1]

So, a part of rejoicing in this light—a part of sharing in this victory feast—must be a pondering of that out of which we come. One of my favorite sayings in all the Bible is Moses' exhortation to the people in Deuteronomy: "Remember the long way that the Lord our God has led you" (8:2).

I would therefore invite us to turn our attention back for a bit to the second of our scripture lessons we heard this night: the story of the sacrifice of Isaac. Now, while we catch our breaths for a moment at the prospect of doing so, we need to admit that this has to be one of the most disorienting, dislocating passages in all of the Holy Scriptures: truly, a deeply disturbing text.

Its interpreters across the centuries haven't been fully confident in knowing what to do with it. To say the least. Yet for Jews and Christians alike, it's been a locus of particular theological fascination and struggle. And from Christian antiquity it's been included in the long lineup of readings from which we hear at the Easter Vigil.

Some scholars suggest that an original source for the story may be an explanation account of why ancient Israel, unlike its neighbors, did *not* practice child sacrifice. But, frankly, this doesn't help us that much in getting a grip on it, as it is set in the book of Genesis. Even beside the horror of it, what sense can we make of it? Isaac is the long-awaited child of promise: promised by God, nonetheless. Isaac is the one through whom God is going to make good on his commitment to Abraham: to establish a posterity through whom the nations will be blessed. To his aged parents—"as good as dead," as the Scriptures memorably put it (Rom 4:19, Heb 11:12)—his birth was miraculous.

---

1. *Hymnal 1982*, #186.

And then, and then:

> God tested Abraham. He said to him, "Abraham!" And he said, "Here I am." He said, "Take your son, your only son Isaac, whom you love, and go to the land of Moriah, and offer him there as a burnt offering on one of the mountains that I shall show you." (Gen 22:2)

What kind of test is this? What kind of deity would ask for it? Why should Abraham have to have been plunged into such an abyss? We realize, in a moment of spiritual vertigo, that the questions are *unanswerable*—at least neither by us nor for us.

However, we have to ponder. We are *meant* to ponder, question, struggle with the text; especially this: Where is God, *really*, to be found in the story?

Our faith tradition honors human reason. It's a part of how we appropriate the gift of faith. But reason, by itself, will not always take us where we need to go. And where reason falls short, interpretive imagination may help. Oddly enough, Christian reflection on this passage has often found God imaged, paradoxically, not so much in the commanding voice, nor even so much in the intervening angel, but in the figures of both Abraham and Isaac themselves.

Both Abraham and Isaac themselves have been seen as "types" of the God who binds himself to *us*—who gives self, utterly, for *us*—even to the point of what fleshly, merely reasonable eyes have to see as the brutally purposeless death of Jesus on the cross.

Faith leads us to a deeper seeing. From the heart of this horrific story that can never "make sense," we are somehow given the assurance of God's utter identification with his people. In Christ, God has chosen to hurtle himself, with Abraham—the father of all who believe—into the abyss.

More than this: in God's Son, Jesus, crucified for us, God has become the *bottom* of the bottomless abyss. And yet more: because death could never hold the One Who Is Life captive, he is risen—and in him we too are being raised.

Descending from Mount Moriah, Abraham comes to know that God's promise is—and will always remain—sheer gift, absolute gift, beyond all possible human claiming, found in the purpose of God. In the resurrection light, we too may see that we're living, now, by that wondrous gift.

Descending from Moriah, Isaac (representing, as well, the people yet to come from him) is now, utterly and manifestly, God's possession: living

"The Binding of God?"

solely by God's grace, entrusted to God's will. In resurrection light, we too may now see—even if it be, still for a time, in partial measure.

We too may now see that we belong to the God who is *with us*—with us even in the midst of intolerable contradictions and vulnerabilities; that this God holds us—and *will* hold us—in Life; and that we may indeed live by our God's grace and trust our God's will.

On the Mount of the Lord Jesus, crucified and raised from death, "it [has been] provided" (Gen 22:14).

Alleluia! Christ is risen!

"The Benefit of Knowing That We Are Sinners"

Year C, Proper 20: 1 Tim 1:15–16

Sunday, September 16, 2007

I OUGHT TO WARN you that this is going to be an *evangelistic* sermon.

Unfortunately, the word "evangelical" has been somewhat compromised. For many these days, all too often it seems to bring to mind such things as rigid life patterns, constricted biblical interpretation, and narrow political agendas. However, all Christians are responsible to reclaim the word. It's a wonderful, classic word after all, coming from the Greek word for "gospel": *good news*. And in spite of what has sometimes seems to have happened with it (on the American religious scene, especially), it's both an honorable title and an important stream of Christian tradition. This is particularly so in the context of Anglican experience. I believe it critical in present times that Episcopalians—across our spectrum—reclaim and re-apply this dimension of our identity. In this sermon, an evangelistic appeal will be set before you.

There: warning duly offered!

In today's lesson from First Timothy, we heard:

> "The saying is sure and worthy of full acceptance, that Christ Jesus came into the world to save sinners—of whom I am the foremost."
> (1:15)

This is language rather foreign to modern sensibilities of devotion. Yes, there are some potential risks to penitential piety. And certainly, such piety *has* been misused in the course of Christian history. Its principal risk is that it can lead us right back to the self-absorption we were trying to

"The Benefit of Knowing That We Are Sinners"

leave behind—an unhealthy loop leading to more entrenched isolation. An inverse narcissism—a narcissism working through pain rather than pleasure—is still narcissism! Furthermore, to be honest, penitential piety has sometimes been abused by the church as a means of manipulating its people.

Nevertheless, acknowledgement of our sinfulness, and also acknowledgement of our call to ongoing repentance, are an undeniable part of our faith. It's not for nothing that almost every Episcopal worship service includes a confession of sin.

Whether it feels congenial to us or not, we find ourselves directed to engage with a kind of "spirituality" in which today's Scripture makes sense: "The saying is sure and worthy of full acceptance, that Christ Jesus came into the world to save sinners—of whom I am the foremost." Far from being a passage tucked out of the way, this verse has been much used in Christian devotion. John Bunyan, the great Puritan writer, paraphrased it for the title of his spiritual autobiography, *Grace Abounding to the Chief of Sinners*.

Language like this is no mere rhetorical flourish. However, it does not mean that we have to try to convince ourselves that we're personally worse than the likes of Hitler, Stalin, Pol Pot, or Osama Bin Laden. We're not talking here about comparative spiritual evaluation. Here's what this kind of language is meant to mean: If we're at all spiritually awake, we should be more acutely aware of *our* depths than we are of the depths of any others. That is, we should be more aware of our *own* delusion, egoism, hurtfulness, and betrayals than those we're able to perceive in others. If the *worst* in us were isolated, enshrined, empowered, and able "to get away with it"—who knows what we'd be capable of? Lord, have mercy—on us, and on those around us.

There are, therefore, very real *benefits* to knowing ourselves to be sinners. It is to these benefits that I invite us to direct our attention this morning. However, before proceeding any further, before we look at any specific benefits, we should affirm that knowing ourselves to be sinners is worth it, first of all, simply because it is the *truth*. Truth is always worth knowing in itself. Or maybe, we might better say, "Truth is always worth knowing, in *himself*." Did not Jesus say, "I *am* the way, and the truth, and the life"? (John 14:6).

In any case, truth is always worth knowing, completely apart from our immediate assessments of congeniality, helpfulness, or advantage. That we might experience truth as "beneficial" is really a bonus—we might say, a *fringe* benefit. The truth, specifically the One Who Is The Truth, *is* our ultimately loving benefit.

So we continue with our theme: the benefits of knowing ourselves to be sinners. I'll set these forward under the headings of five particular *capacities*.

The *first* benefit that I would name (and I'm saving the best one for last) is the *capacity of seeing how ourselves contribute to situations that we don't like*—instead of just blaming or judging others. How quickly, how firmly, we seize on to the partial fault of those with whom we are in some difficulty—so we can lay to *their* account all the blame. There's a real relief we can feel when we've played a successful round of the "gotcha!" game. *We're* safe; we're off the hook. Yet each time we pull this off, there's a little less of us, deep down. Our souls are diminished. We have indulged in another little bit of non-life. There's a painfully insightful line in Dostoevsky's *Brothers Karamazov*, spoken by the saintly Elder Zosima:

> "It sometimes feels very good to take offense, doesn't it?"[1]

We become infatuated with our "victim status." Ironically, when human beings are swept up by notions of our own victimhood—either personal or corporate—it is precisely *then* that we can be at our most injurious, most unjust, most hurtful. So, the capacity of seeing our own contributions to the sinful mix of fault and fallibility can be nothing less than life-saving.

The *second* benefit of knowing ourselves to be sinners that I'm setting before us may be a little more complicated. At least, we often make it more complicated. Please bear with me for a little bit, before I summarize it. This benefit allows us to be not nearly so likely of habitually reducing—or habitually discounting—the good things done for us to merely the unremarkable payment of what we have coming to us anyway—while viewing anything other than what we deem "the best" as an outrage. To put it more simply: this is a benefit that allows us to be *at least* twice more likely to say "thank you" than to complain. Now, to summarize it: knowing ourselves to be sinners notably increases our *capacity of appreciation and gratitude* in an imperfect world in which it will always be possible to find some fault.

Now, proceeding to the *third* benefit, which I'd say is the *capacity of sharing concerns* with our fellow sinners, when we need to do so, gently and affirmingly—and with the least needful amount of applied force. Using

---

1. Dostoevsky, *Brothers Karamazov* (Pevear and Volokhonsky; pt. 1, bk. 2, ch. 2 "The Old Buffoon"), 44.

"The Benefit of Knowing That We Are Sinners"

more than really needful force in personal conflict is inherently sinful. By so doing we become men and women "of violence."

The flip side of this is the ability to *receive* expressions of concerns well: that is, non-reactively, non-dismissively, giving the benefit of the doubt—even, and I think this is key here—even when others have not communicated in perfect manner. Again, there's a sadly soul-diminishing relief we can feel when we relate to another like this—even if the words aren't fully articulated: "You didn't express yourself in just the right way. 'Gotcha!' I—or we—don't need to pay any attention to what you were trying to say." Such a move can be very effective for the agenda of ego-protection—protecting what we think we want. But it's also isolating and corrosive. However, graciously for us sinners, another way of relating in the midst of conflict has been opened to us. Being able to really hear others usually goes right along with a healthy level of self-suspicion.

Going on to the *fourth* benefit: in knowing ourselves to be sinners we find the *capacity of being forgiving*. This forgiveness business will always be one of the greater challenges in living out our faith. "Forgive us our trespasses, *as we forgive* those who trespass against us," as we pray all the time in the Lord's Prayer. It should be more of an attention-getter than it usually is. That "as we forgive" bit; maybe we ought to find that more worrisome than we do! Of course, we're not talking about trying to purchase God's forgiveness by "working up" our own forgiving! That would be desperate enterprise, doomed to fail. What the prayer *does* teach us is that we can't really be receiving the forgiveness that comes from God unless we're *also* passing it on to others.

We get confused about forgiveness. It isn't denial, or minimization, or enabling. Neither is it some sort of emotional certification that the other has "fixed" things to our satisfaction. Forgiveness means *remission* of debt. Sometimes, in this world of ours, dealing with grave trespass, we may have to speak of "release" rather than "remission." But in either case, with different ramifications for where the relationship goes from there, in forgiveness we say to another, "I am no longer going to live as your creditor."

And in all cases, our own forgiving is uniquely enabled in our lively awareness that we are sinners; that if before the face of God, we were dependent on our own earning or fixing, we would be in big trouble.

Paradoxically, a part of this capacity of forgiveness is an appropriate measure of self-compassion (grounded, of course, in *God's* mercy).

In this—or rather, in *him*—we are freed from the human-based, human-centered perfectionism with which we can so often afflict ourselves.

None of this means that we're nonchalant in regard to sin. We're not at all talking about the caricature of faith in Christ that W. H. Auden puts on the lips of Herod in *For the Time Being*. "Every crook will argue: 'I like committing crimes. God likes forgiving them. Really the world is admirably arranged.'"[2] Rather, the right way of looking at sin and forgiveness involves authentic knowledge of who we are, where we are, and where we are going—all of which rests, first of all, on the knowledge of God.

Which brings us, now, to the *last of our five*, the best for last—or, with greater spiritual accuracy, the first for last: in faith, with the knowledge that we are sinners, we are given the *capacity to know*—and to know ever more deeply—*that God has forgiven us*. Out of this gracious knowledge comes our following ability to ask and to receive forgiveness from one another.

Seeing how *we* contribute to situations we don't like, appreciation and gratitude in an imperfect world, gentleness and affirmation even in conflict, being forgiving, receiving forgiveness, sinners that we are. Such knowledge, such benefits, such capacities are from God: the gifts of God for the people of God.

We find, at the end, that this penitential piety we initially may have found off-putting—may have resisted—is not debilitating but *empowering*. This last week I ran across a striking quote. Here it is: "Repentance is not . . . self-loathing. Repentance is insight."[3]

"Repentance is insight." So, we're never to lose heart. If crushed by the weight of all that is lacking—all that is amiss, we are to know that Christ came precisely for the likes of us. More than this; even in our brokenness, with healing almost always incrementally manifested, *we* become signs of grace, instruments of redemption in this needy world.

> "The saying is sure and worthy of full acceptance, that Christ Jesus came into the world to save sinners—of whom I am the foremost. But for that very reason I received mercy, so that in me, as the foremost, Jesus Christ might display the utmost patience, making me an example to those who would come to believe in him for eternal life. To the King of the ages, immortal, invisible, the only God, be honor and glory forever and ever." (1:15–17)

---

2. Auden, *For the Time Being*, 57 ("The Massacre of the Innocents").
3. Frederica Matthews-Green, cited in Rutledge, *Not Ashamed of the Gospel*, 336.

"The Benefit of Knowing That We Are Sinners"

I'll conclude with a question, respectfully addressed to each one present: Dear fellow sinner, how goes it? Do you yet know? In Jesus of Nazareth, the Word of God, dwelling among us, in this Lord crucified and raised from death, do you yet know that grace has abounded for *you*, the chief of sinners?

"The Table with the Open Space"
Trinity Sunday

June 7, 2009

TODAY IS THE CONCLUSION of the two great cycles in the church year which are devoted to presenting the Christ event: first, Christ's advent and epiphany; then Christ's life, death, resurrection, glorification: the sending of the Spirit.

In the following months, until the end of November, the appointed readings will focus more on our response to the gospel message. But today, we conclude with the great theme of the Holy Trinity; in the classic words—One God, glorified in Three Persons: Father, Son, and Spirit; as we have been so graced to name.

Trinitarian doctrine is the crown of Christian theology. Yet many have found it an intimidating doctrine—and rightly so! But perhaps it isn't such a bad thing to be theologically intimidated! Especially in reference to divinity, we ought to remember that all human words must be inadequate. Regrettably, we have to admit that far too often, Christians have behaved as though our theological speaking not only expressed truth but was *itself* the truth.

But God remains God—and it is God himself who is ultimate truth. This being the case, "truth" must be utterly beyond our human capturing and control: "ineffable, inconceivable, invisible, incomprehensible."[1]

Regrettably, theological language has sometimes been used as an ending to thought: a mere boundary. However, I believe that the authentic purpose of these classic words of faith is the indication of a center from which we engage in an on-going life. Theology has something in common

---

1. Preface, "The Anaphora," *Divine Liturgy of Saint John Chrysostom*, in Hapgood, *Service Book*, 101.

with a map. Both can only very partially describe the realities they seek to represent. And even a grand collection of well-preserved maps will do us very little good unless we set out to our destination. Merely "correct" yet empty recitation of once life-giving formulas can be spiritually injurious.

Nevertheless, especially if the trip is important, a map can be a valuable thing indeed. We can admit the limitation and humanity of our cartographers and still be most grateful for their work. Somehow, astoundingly, we can and we must speak—because God has spoken to us first.

As a key affirmation, Christianity recognizes a radical and ongoing otherness between what we are and what God is. However, in the Christian tradition, the transcendent is not insulated away from the world, as though the cosmos were some gigantic spiritual bureaucracy. In contrast to a number of dualistic approaches, Christianity posits the closest involvement of the spiritual with the physical.

That which is radically "other" is also closer to us than our hearts. The transcendent one has broken through to us.

> "We declare . . . what was from the beginning, what we have heard, what we have seen with our eyes, what we have looked at and touched with our hands, concerning the word of life." (1 John 1:1)

In spite of the weakness of language, we speak theologically because in the Person of Jesus Christ we encounter a greater and ultimately defining experience—an experience not merely private but meant to be shared in community—an experience which has joined us into new relationship not only with God, but with the world.

Our faith is rooted in incarnation. We find, in the pattern of Christ's own self, "treasure . . . in earthen vessels" (2 Cor 4:7 KJV)—the perfect expressed through the limited, the divine manifested in the profoundly human. So too it is with the words of faith.

In a world afflicted with alienation and fragmentation, it was necessary that divine unity be a primary message. "Hear, O Israel; [hear, O people:] the Lord our God, the Lord is one" (Mark 12:29; Deut 6:4). "We believe in *one* God."

The New Testament reiterates this resoundingly—and also leads us to express more. The mystery of Christ was key in the development of Trinitarian doctrine. In him—in this Person—we encounter one in full unity with our own humanity but also the one who exists from all time, as God. He is, in himself, the mediator between God and humankind, the one in whom we are restored to nothing less than divine life. Therefore, the church

"The Table with the Open Space"

offers its affirmation, in the words of the Nicene Creed, that Jesus is the "Son of God . . . of one Being with the Father."[2]

Likewise, we encounter the presence of the Spirit, proceeding from the Father (John 15:26) and sent as the seal of the Son's work. As Spirit actualizes the Christ-life in us, we are enabled to acknowledge that it too, "with the Father and the Son . . . is [to be] worshipped and glorified." From a mystery of shared and lived faith, and, once again, realizing the poverty of words, we nevertheless make a startling affirmation: at the heart of the one truth, a relationship is revealed.

So: there is something *inherently relational* in the nature of ultimate reality.

This, by the way, is one of the reasons why the increasingly popular replacement of the classic formula "Father, Son, and Holy Spirit"—which is entirely biblical, and also so central in the church's unbroken historic tradition—with things like "Creator, Redeemer, and Sustainer," is such a bad idea. It replaces *Persons* with what can be understood just as easily as mere functions or modes of the Godhead.

Such a collapsing of Persons into functions also forgets the truth in the classic theological maxim "the external works of the Trinity are undivided."[3] In spite of some divine activities being especially associated with one of the Persons of the Trinity, *all divine activity toward us is Triune: the action of the entire Godhead.* So, Son and Spirit are also involved in creation, the Father and the Spirit in redemption, and the Father and the Son in sanctification.

So, no: the replacement formulas—even if put forward with good intentions—just won't do. I find that I must say, along with Gregory of Nazianzus—the fourth-century bishop and one of the greatest theologians in the history of the church,

"When I say, 'God,' I mean Father and Son and Holy Spirit."[4]

There is something inherently *relational*—and something *personal-in-relationship*—in the nature of ultimate reality.

This profoundly informs how we see ourselves. Perhaps encouraged by our culture's infatuation with individualism, we certainly have a way of seeing the demands of our relationships as an interruption—or perhaps even a threat. Haven't we been told that everyone pursuing his or her own

---

2. "τὸν Υἱὸν τοῦ Θεοῦ...ὁμοούσιον τῷ Πατρί." *Book of Common Prayer*, 358.
3. See Augustine, *Trinity* 1.2.7–8 (Hill, 69–70).
4. Gregory of Nazianzus, *Festal Orations* 38.8 (Harrison, 66).

separate good (economic or political or otherwise) is the very "engine" which will produce an earthly paradise? "I'll take care of myself first, then everyone else gets what's left."

But what if the demands on our separateness, these interruptions of our own agendas, were the stuff of life itself? If we affirm that persons cannot be reduced to functions or commodities—if we affirm an eternal community within divine being, and we also say that we are made "in the image and likeness" of God (Gen 1:27, 5:2), are we not then made for life in communion?

As much as human language is inevitably limited in expressing Trinitarian doctrine, iconographic presentation involves even more challenges. No one "has seen the Father" (John 6:46), and the Spirit is Spirit. Sometimes in the Christian visual arts we find symbolic representations such as intersecting circles. Most of us are familiar with the representation containing the three images of an old man, a younger man, and a bird. While previous ages would have also understood the risks and benefits of any visual effort, more recently—and with some good reason, many have an increased sense of the confusion associated with this well-known image.

But there is another icon, rather different, which I personally find both artistically beautiful and theologically profound. This is the representation painted by Andrei Rublev, the great medieval Russian iconographer. I invite you now to direct your attention to the copy provided. Please take a few moments to begin to do so.

Rublev makes no attempt to portray the Trinity directly. Rather, he uses an event from the Abraham story as a sort of visual allegory. The event is Abraham's hospitality to the three mysterious visitors who announced the birth of Isaac (Gen 18:1–8). Rublev's image is remarkably simple: three figures seated at a table. The figures are in human likeness but ambiguous. From the viewer's perspective, the Person of the Father is on the left, with a hand of direction for the next figure in the middle position. The middle figure represents the Son, whose acceptance and accomplishment of the Father's mission is shown by a slightly inclined head and by a hand outstretched, where one sees, at the center, the bread of offering. The right-hand figure, the Spirit, equal—and to us, the most ambiguous of the Three—yet also with a hand extended, co-involved in the redemptive movement. If one looks at the outline of the three figures, one sees, subtly yet clearly, that they form a circle: the unity and perfection of the Trinity

"The Table with the Open Space"

from all eternity. And yet perhaps most strikingly, these three do not take up all the space at their table.

As we meditate on the icon, we can perceive *another* circle, even more subtle: one implied in its composition, that extends out from the icon's surface to include the viewer! To catch it, look at the heads of the three figures. Do you start to see it?

The Trinity, eternally perfect in itself, calls us likewise into being. And at the icon's nearest side, notice that an open place has been left for us: "Join us at the table of life!" Now ponder further the shape of that open space. Rather like a chalice, isn't it?

The transcendent God—who is radically "other"—both creates and redeems us that we may share in a glorious fellowship: a fellowship of communion with God, with one another, and with all creation. This is what is means to be baptized into the people who bear the name of the Trinity: Father, Son, and Spirit. In some more of those classic theological words, we say that what belongs to Christ by nature now—in the work of God—is given to us by grace:

> "For all who are led by the Spirit of God are children of God. For you did not receive a spirit of slavery to fall back into fear, but you have received a spirit of adoption. When we cry, 'Abba! Father!' it is that very Spirit bearing witness to our spirit that we are children of God, and if children, then heirs, heirs of God and joint heirs with Christ." (Rom 8:14–17a)

"But We See Jesus"
Church of the Holy Spirit, Orleans, Massachusetts

Year B, Proper 22: Hebrews 1:1–4; 2:5–12
October 4, 2009
First Sermon as Rector

THE ANONYMOUS LETTER TO the Hebrews is an enigmatic piece of writing. We're not even sure that it's really a letter as such. Some have thought that it might be a very early Christian sermon. Frankly, much of it now seems rather arcane, its imagery distant. But its central message is enduringly relevant, speaking very directly to our hearts and our condition. We'll be hearing portions from Hebrews as Sunday's second lesson for the better part of the next two months. Today, we begin with the beginning:

> "Long ago, God spoke to our ancestors in many and various ways by the prophets, but in these last days, he has spoken to us by a Son." (1:1–2)

So Jesus Christ is what God has to say to us: God's primal, fulfilling, and final Word. This speaking addresses us—as persons on a great journey, which began when we were uttered into being. As we know too well, our journey includes a falling into sin's captivity but also a deliverance from that captivity—by that same One by whom we were spoken into being. Yet we're still travelling with a long way to go, with so much in store. And—as we also know all too well—this is a pilgrimage now very much bound up with suffering.

The key message of the letter to the Hebrews is that on this journey, we are not travelling alone. Jesus is the meeting place: the meeting place of who God is and who we are—and who we are becoming. More than this, Jesus, the Son, has travelled our path—on our terms—as our brother, and we as his sisters and brothers. So he shares our suffering and has shared our death. Through this, he becomes the pioneer (we might say, the trailblazer) of our salvation. We are not travelling this journey of ours alone, and now "by him, and with him, and in him,"[1] it's a journey with a purpose.

As we proceed on the way, our text invites us to ponder this present in-between reality of ours. Sometimes we sprint. Much more often, we trudge along with a few pauses now and then to catch our breath and sometimes, as well, a questionable detour or two. God can handle all of it. More than this, God in Christ Jesus is with us through all of it.

Our recognition of God is imperfect, or sometimes even minimal. Yet unlike us, God doesn't seem to be too troubled by not always getting due credit. In the here and now, God is often working anonymously. God's presence, God's grace, God's purpose; these are greater than all our stuff. That's what—that's *who* we meet in God's Son, Jesus.

Now to heighten our focus a bit more specifically, I'd like to ponder the curious phrase in our text,

"But we do see Jesus." (2:9)

This is an assurance after the candid recognition of all that we do *not* presently see while we're on the way—all the "not yet" of God's good purpose for us. Experience leads us to acknowledge that in this present life we see plenty of things distinctly counter to our hopes for the "not yet." Nevertheless, in response, the author of Hebrews says in response,

"We do see Jesus."

This is a curious phrase, because by every evident, present recognition of ours, we *don't* see him. By every usual perception, Jesus is now gone. Even this morning's passage references the mystery of Christ's ascension:

"When he had made purification for sins, he sat down at the right hand of the majesty on high." (1:3)

Christ is risen. Christ lives. But somehow in ways that human language, even human sacred language, can barely begin to indicate, Christ's present life has been translated out of the sphere of our present perception.

As with all metaphors, thinking of heaven as "up there" has its limits. Don't get me wrong. I delight in metaphor. There's no other way we humans apprehend anything (in science as well as poetry). Nevertheless, we have to

---

1. "The Great Thanksgiving," Doxology, in *Book of Common Prayer*, 363, 369.

be very careful, I think, with a too-exclusive reliance on "up" or "upwards" to indicate heaven. The heavenly reality can also sometimes be indicated in metaphors of deep within, or close alongside—just out of sight.

But how does this help us take hold of our text's assurance that we do see Jesus? We're talking about a different kind of perception: a Spirit-given, Spirit-enabled perception—manifested to us in unexpected forms. How do we see in this way? How do we encounter the unexpected company for whom we've been waiting all along?

First of all, it's a gift. A gift, not an achievement. "Grace" is a keyword—maybe the keyword—in our spiritual vocabulary, and "by the grace of God" is the indispensable concept. This vision is a gift to be received, never a conjuring up. As grace is really grace and God is really God, so grace can mercifully exploit the slightest fissures to penetrate our best and most hardened defenses. Thanks be. More than this, I believe that divine grace can create its *own* fissures to get past our well-fortified layers of delusional security. The concept of grace is so important because in the end, if things ultimately depended on our own good sense, we'd all be in big trouble.

Of course, it is also a healthy, practical, spiritually productive thing to hold ourselves—and to grow—so to be better receivers of the gift. At least provisionally, we can either impede or welcome the unexpected vision of Christ. What impedes? What clouds over our spiritual sight? Habitual irritation, pervasive anxiety, indulging in the pursuit of control. All those sorts of strategies through which we seek to manage and protect our existence.

And what might serve to welcome the sight of Jesus? A well-spoken saying comes to mind. "Let go, and let God." There's a powerful liberation in store for us when we realize that we no longer have to try to carry out God's job description. "Let go, and let God."

Welcoming the vision of Christ means, then, a willingness to receive, a willingness to be led, recovering the capacity for surprise, embracing the reality and freedom of not having to have things all figured out, bearing with (and even learning to delight in) paradox. We're speaking here of a spiritual adventuresomeness; getting past our resistance to launching out into the risky depths. Above all, we're speaking of the growing capacity of seeing what we did not expect to see.

But we do see Jesus. Notice the present tense. Here and now on this side of the great divide between the "already" and the "not yet." Maybe this is a vision given through our everyday seeing of one another. Those dear to us, those who warm our hearts, but also those who frustrate us, those who get in the way of what we think we want and need. This vision is given in the sight of both those who comfort us and also those who stretch us far beyond our comfort zones.

It goes without saying that the frustrating and the uncomfortable people are very often those who need the help we are in a position to give. Sometimes, that's a simple and as difficult as really paying attention.

> "Lord, when was it that we saw *you*?" . . . "Truly I tell you, just as you did it to one of the least of these, you did it to me." (Matt 25:37, 40)

Now to take this yet another step, still to be named—though we name it with all due caution. Occasionally, we are given brief, partial, and paradoxical glimpses of Jesus even in our own poor selves. And lest we be swamped, utterly swamped by this, we remember again that such a vision is no desperate conjuring on our own part, no strained forcing out of our tired eyes.

Remember grace. Remember the Giver. Through all our growth and all our evasions, through progress and interruptions, grace will lead us home. Surely now, we see dimly. By grace, then we will see face-to-face. We will come to see fully, even as we had been fully seen (1 Cor 13:12). As it is put in one of my favorite Christmas hymns, "Once in Royal David's City,"

> And our eyes at last shall see him through his own redeeming love
> . . . he leads his children on to the place where he has gone.[2]

Meanwhile, our Lord incrementally accustoms our perception to greater measures of his light. *Incrementally*: that can be a challenge for us—but we need to bear with what we often deem to be God's inefficiency. All-or-nothing thinking is both unrealistic and colossally unhelpful, and we are usually being called to greater measures of patience: patience with one another, with ourselves, and with God, too.

It has been mentioned that I have a particular love of poetry, and so I do. One of my favorites is Gerard Manley Hopkins, a nineteenth-century English poet who was also a Jesuit priest. There's a particular poem of his that speaks to me on this occasion, and, in closing, I'd like to share it with you now. As we are carried in its rich imagery, I hope that its aptness for us today will become evident.

---

2. *Hymnal 1982*, #102.

From the East Gate

As kingfishers catch fire, dragonflies draw flame;
As tumbled over rim in roundy wells
Stones ring; like each tucked string tells, each hung bell's
Bow swung finds tongue to fling out broad its name;
Each mortal thing does one thing and the same:
Deals out that being indoors each one dwells;
Selves—goes itself; *myself* it speaks and spells,
Crying *What I do is me: for that I came.*

I say more: the just man justices;
Keeps gráce: that keeps all his goings graces;
Acts in God's eye what in God's eye he is—
Christ—for Christ plays in ten thousand places,
Lovely in limbs, and lovely in eyes not his
To the Father through the features of men's faces.[3]

---

3. Hopkins, *Poems and Prose*, 51.

"The Taste for Heaven"

The Fourth Sunday After Easter, Year C: Rev 7:9–17

April 21, 2013
The Sunday Following the Boston Marathon Bombing

THIS LAST MONDAY AFTERNOON, at about ten minutes before three, once again we were swept up in horrible, unimaginable violence. That violence and its aftermath are hard to bear—and hard to bear *spiritually*, in particular. We are overwhelmed—with dismay, with fear, with anger, with deep questioning. But in the midst of the terrible happenings, we also have a humbled gratitude for those who stepped forward into spheres of great danger, to tend to the wounded, to comfort the dying, to be present with the bereaved, and to secure our safety.

We're here together this morning, drawn by the Spirit, asking questions, and taking hold of such threads of hope as are given to us. And maybe that's what matters most of all today. Yesterday, I was asked—in short order—about capital punishment, pacifism, and the universality of forgiveness. Well, I probably won't have very good answers. We're all struggling, aren't we?

Before going on, though, maybe I need to offer a brief comment about forgiveness. It is, indeed, the unbroken proclamation of the church that God's forgiveness is sufficient to deal with every manner of sin, even the most terrible. But we take hold of God's forgiveness; we connect with its wonderful reality, through repentance and faith. However, if we are outraged at the very notion that we *need* to be forgiven, if we thereby hold the Giver in contempt and refuse the gift—we still have a major problem. Forgiveness is grace, not magic.

From the East Gate

Long before last Monday, I had planned to preach on the passage from Revelation that we just heard. Of course, I had no idea then how strangely apt its language might be for us today.

We'll launch in, now, with a quick reminder that the whole book of Revelation is highly symbolic. It's extended poetry—and we can't take hold of what the Spirit means to give to us in this strange book unless we can apprehend it with *poetic diction*.[1] It's a highly repetitive book—with flashbacks and flash-forwards increasing in intensity, the scene shifting back and forward between heaven and earth. It's filled with extravagant imagery, resonating with many biblical allusions, many of which we now barely "get." But as all this poetry sweeps over us and seeps into us, perhaps we will "hear what the Spirit [is saying]" (2:7). May it be so.

What's the message? In one word: "God."

It's about God. From first to last: Alpha and Omega. It's about the real God who is infinitely more than an extension of ourselves, a God who is irreducibly "other." This is the God who can be intimidating—whom we would often rather avoid when things don't feel quite so high-stakes but nevertheless—at deepest down level—the God we know we need at crunch time. More than this: that great, irreducibly "other" God cares—from his very heart of love and mercy—about *us*.

Yet a difficult honesty has to admit that much of the time it doesn't feel as though this is so. In the world where you and I live, often—maybe more often than not—God can feel distant and disconnected. We wonder, "Where *are* you?" In his time, Jesus wondered that too, didn't he?

Emily Dickinson is one of the English language's greatest poets. She was not a conventional believer, that's for sure, but she certainly conveyed human experience powerfully—especially our struggle with faith. One of her poems came to mind for me in this last week. I'd like to share it with you:

> Apparently with no surprise,
> To any happy flower,
> The frost beheads it at its play,
> In accidental power.
> The blond assassin passes on.
> The sun proceeds unmoved,
> To measure off another day,
> For an approving God.[2]

---

1. Allusion, here, to Owen Barfield's *Poetic Diction*.
2. Dickinson, *Complete Poems*, 667–68.

"The Taste for Heaven"

Yes. It sometimes feels that way, doesn't it? And yet, with all due respect to Dickinson, the poetry of the Holy Spirit given to us in the book of Revelation sets forth an even *greater* reality: more than our eyes can now perceive and more than our present can possibly hold.

To be sure, this doesn't "make it all better" right away. It doesn't immediately answer all the questions. But as we keep putting one foot in front of the other in this broken world of ours, and with these broken hearts, this strange utterance of the Spirit recasts all things. "Behold, I make all things new" (21:5 KJV, RSV).

Throughout the book of Revelation—and centrally in today's text—we find the theme of *worship*. For God's people, it is worship which connects our present, still-broken earthly reality with the heavenly. Now, we ought to be clear about what worship is and what it isn't. It is *not* as though the Almighty God is of such terribly weak ego strength that he has to be flattered constantly to build up his sense of self. No, *God* doesn't need our worship. It is *we* who need to worship—in order to be attuned to reality. We aren't speaking here of mere ritual in itself but rather—as God's people—the adoration, the delight, the obedience and full response of our life to our holy and worship-worthy God.

We must never buy into the notion that this is some sort of corporate indulgence on the part of the church, a diversion from our other, "really important" business. That may be how the world would like to see it. We must not. Rather, the worship of God—Father, Son, and Holy Spirit—is always our first duty and our culminating joy as God's people. Everything else we do flows out from it—and leads back to it in turn. This is what connects us, here and now, to heaven. This is what attunes us to reality.

> "After this I looked, and there was a great multitude that no one could count, from every nation, from all tribes and peoples and languages, standing before the throne and before the Lamb, robed in white, with palm branches in their hands. They cried out in a loud voice, saying, 'Salvation belongs to our God who is seated on the throne, and to the Lamb!' And all the angels stood around the throne and around the elders and the four living creatures, and they fell on their faces before the throne and worshipped." (7:9–11)

In most popular thinking about the world to come, we focus on the question: Who "gets" to *go* to heaven? This ignores the deeper—perhaps much more critical—issue of whether we would like it very much if we *were* there!³ Imagine "heaven" as a great, eternal, cosmic celebration. But suppose, for the sake of illustration, that we really didn't like being around the others who were invited, suppose we found the activities unpleasant, and—finally—didn't care much for the Host, the One around whom it all was gathered. There's nowhere "else" to go, and it's never going to end. We might have a rather different word than "heaven" for that experience, mightn't we?

Something to think about.

So how do we get to the "there" about which we've been speaking—and recognize it as a blessing? How do we get to the intersection with eternal joy? That's the question which the seer of Revelation poses himself. Who are those summoned to this adoration and saving delight?

> 'Who are these, robed in white, and where have they come from?' I said to him, 'Sir, you are the one that knows.' Then he said to me, 'These are they who have come out of the great ordeal; they have washed their robes and made them white in the blood of the Lamb.' (7:13–14)

We know a little more—maybe a good deal more—about "ordeal" this last week: both the outwardly traumatic and also the quiet sufferings of the heart with which our life is now bound up.

> These are they who have come out of the great ordeal; they have washed their robes and made them white in the blood of the Lamb.'

This isn't *only* just for the future, although it is certainly future in significant part. These words also testify to a *present* reality: sharing in the victory of God, born into the delight of God, even *here and now*—when we don't have answers to questions we so desperately seek. And we get to this reality, both present and future, through the sacrifice of Jesus.

It is through the self-emptying of God incarnate, in the blood of the Lamb, that we are born into the reality of worship and adoration. It is through Christ's redemptive sacrifice on the cross that we are able to stand before the eternal throne.

---

3. My thinking behind this question has been focused in particular through the writings of Isaac the Syrian (both *The Ascetical Homilies* and 'The Second Part,' Chapters *IV-XLI*). Dostoevsky channels the relevant teachings in the *Homilies* through the Elder Zosima's character in *Brothers Karamazov* (Pevear and Volokhonsky; pt. 2, bk. 6, ch. 3 "From Talks and Homilies of the Elder Zosima"), 318–20, 322–24. Additionally, I found Dallas Willard's comments in his *Allure of Gentleness* to be insightful and exceptionally well-put (*Allure of Gentleness*, 67–70). And of course C. S. Lewis' *The Great Divorce* is invaluable in profoundly—and vividly—reframing the question.

"The Taste for Heaven"

So, while we are involved—with the totality of our being—worship is not our separate human project. It is based, at the root of it, on who God is and what God does.

That's where we begin—always. And where does a life of worship *lead*? It leads to God. Alpha and Omega. Worship leads us back to the provision which God gives—to the care in which God holds us: more than our eyes can now see and more than our present can now hold. Ultimately (even though we must wait for a time), a life of worship leads us to the redemption of *all* suffering.

From first to last, it's about God. Only because of this do we matter in turn. If it weren't about God, if we were just slogging it out in a universe of happenstance, then we would pass away into insignificance. But because of the real God, we matter. Yes, God is at work—with nothing less than cosmic redemption. God is concerned for the character and quality of human community. But we matter. You and I matter. *Personally*. We are infinitely more than mere raw material for some collective utopia. Our joys, our aspirations, our failures, the burdens of our hearts—we matter.

We hear in the text, "God will wipe away every tear." I thought of Psalm 56, too, which speaks to the same theme:

> O God, you put my tears in your bottle. Are they not in your record? (56:8)

Yes. God cares for the great and the global. But God cares about *you*, too, right now as you sit in the pew—and to eternity. And there's no burden too insignificant—or too big—for the wonderful mercy. So even if we will need to learn to walk in the dark for a while, we carry the light of God implanted by the Spirit in our hearts.

The *habituation* of worship in our lives takes commitment and spiritual discipline. In a world with plenty of distractions, this doesn't just happen. Yet it is *God himself* who gives us the desire and capacity for worship. It is God, through Jesus the Son, in the power of the Spirit, who leads us as we acquire "the taste for heaven" ever more perfectly—then to share it ever more abundantly. This is the hope of God's people:

> The Lamb at the center of the throne will be their shepherd. He will guide them to springs of the water of life, and God will wipe away every tear from their eyes. (7:17)

And so, in the midst of all things; even today—*especially* today:

From the East Gate

Blessing and glory and wisdom and thanksgiving and honor and power and might be to our God forever and ever! Amen. (7:12)

"Stretched"

Third Sunday in Lent, Year A: Rom 5:1–11

February 24, 2014

PHYSICAL THERAPISTS.

Anyone here either been to one—or know someone who has been to one? Raise your hands; raise them high. OK, thank you.

They're *pushy* people and, as they work on us, often certainly don't seem all that nice. They make folks stretch out what doesn't want to be stretched out and to work on that which would rather be left alone. Pushy people.

But physical therapists can do very necessary work for us. Here's the problem: if there's something in us that's hurting, we tend to favor it, pull back, and to use other muscles and other tendons in ways that make the hurting part even weaker and throw our whole body off balance. So these pushy people stretch us out, so that we can get strong and get back in balance.

That's a pretty good metaphor for what God often does in our spiritual life.

Just as in our physical pain we tend to pull in, shut down, to favor one thing, avoid another, and cause ourselves injury, we can do the same in the way of the Spirit. We can hunker down in the comfortable, or what seems to be comfortable. It seems to be working—but we're avoiding all sorts of things that need to be in play. Even experienced Christians can need some serious spiritual therapy. And our good God stretches us out and gets us focusing and working in ways that we would otherwise tend to avoid.

We all have our own particular comfort and avoidance zones. This also seems true for "denominations" or particular Christian traditions as a whole, which have their various styles, approaches, and emphases.

Don't get me wrong; I deeply cherish the Episcopal Church. But there are areas from which we, too, are likely to pull back—just like everybody else, in their own ways: areas that we're inclined to leave alone because, at least to us, maybe they're not the most comfortable territory. So, I'll name a few things that we may be a little too likely to hear in our own particular Christian context.

> "Saint Paul—*don't like* him!"
> "John's Gospel—*hmmm*, really?"
> "Do we *have* to say those creeds?"

And let's not even talk about the doctrines of the cross! Not to be judgmental, but when I when hear things like that frequently enough, I sometimes wonder, "What's left?" Maybe a few excerpts here and there, perhaps valued more for what they are *not* than for what they are.

The truth of the matter is that in our spiritual life we often need to head into the area of discomfort. Not go around it—not evade it—but allow ourselves to get stretched out and see, precisely, in that difficult encounter what gift God may have to give to us.

We may be too likely to pull back when we hit one of our immediate, visceral reactivities. But, a reactive *"I don't like it!"* may not be a very suitable ultimate value judgment. Certainly, making space for a range of interpretations, respecting the place of questions and doubts in the process of faith, are a valued part of our particular Christian tradition. We don't bind ourselves to ridged, wooden, unquestioning literalisms. Nevertheless, we need to admit that sometimes not only our health but our very life may depend on *learning to love what is good for us.*

Maybe those avoided parts are there for a good reason after all. Maybe there's some One else who knows better what we need.

All of which brings us to today's passage from Paul's Letter to the Romans, the fifth chapter, verses one through eleven: let's get past our reactivities, lean in, and see what gifts God may have to give.

> "Since we are justified by faith we have peace with God through our Lord Jesus Christ." (5:1)

Wonderful words but with more than a hint of disquiet in them. You mean, we weren't at peace before? And the passage gets worse:

> "While we were still weak at the right time Christ died for the ungodly." (5:6)

"Ungodly." Who's Paul talking about here?

Even more intense:

> "God proves his love for us, in that while we were still sinners, Christ died for us. Much more surely then, now that we have been justified by his blood will we be saved through him from the wrath of God. For if while we were enemies, we were reconciled to God through the death of his Son much more surely, having been reconciled, will we be saved by his life." (5:8–9)

We were weak; we were sinners; we had even become God's enemies. What possibly could Paul, or the Spirit speaking through Paul, be talking about here?

Is it really that bad? We'd rather think not. There's a part in us that would rather have a non-intimidating, cut-down-to-size kind of god. This is the kind of god we hear about in the false gospel of mere human niceness. It goes something along these lines: we're so nice that this cut-down-to-size god is infatuated with us. We're so nice, this "god" has a *crush* on us.[1]

Well, this sort of thing may feel good for a little while, but deep down we know that that's not the God we need at crunch time. Deep down we know that's not the God we need when the stakes are high and we're facing something terrible: looking at some heartbreaking, unresolved crisis; looking at death, our own or the death of someone we care about more than anybody else in the world. Deep down, we know that the God with both the intention and the ability to deal with anything and everything is the God who *can* be rather intimidating: The God for whom we have to get stretched out—perhaps agonizingly—to meet again.

Here's the problem with thinking that we're so nice that God is infatuated with us—the phony gospel of niceness: we know that we are not entirely that nice. What about the un-nice places? How about the broken and hurting places? How about the miserable places where we've blown it,

---

1. The kind of religiosity I object to here was well-satirized by Flannery O'Connor in an episode from her novel *Wise Blood*, featuring a huckster named Hoover Shoats peddling what he advertises as a new, up-to-date faith that people can buy into for only a dollar. "Not too much to pay to unlock that little rose of sweetness inside you!" Shoats—who at this point in the story is going by the name of Onnie Jay Holy—calls the enterprise "the Church of Christ Without Christ," which he says, when he discovered it, "was going to get a new jesus to help me bring my sweet nature into the open where ever'body could enjoy it" (O'Connor, *Collected Works*, 86, 87). Shoats is a rough, very homespun character, but I find that the attitudes he appeals to can often be found in quite sophisticated, so much more urbane—and much more expensive forms.

where we've *been* hurtful? The "nice" phony god is of no help there. We're on our own if that's the kind of god we have—but that is *not* the kind of God we have.

See, this overwhelmingly intimidating message that we heard in Romans, chapter five, is a message of a God who has a love big enough, deep enough, and can reach far enough as to embrace even the likes of us, no matter what. No matter what!

We were weak; we were sinners; we were even God's enemies. The grace of God we meet in Jesus Christ is big enough and strong enough to reach us even there. No "too far" or no "too deep" or "too hard" for that kind of God: the God we meet in Jesus Christ—"and him crucified" (1 Cor 2:2). This is a God who has not played it safe on the sidelines. This is the God who has met, who has embraced, who has shared, who has experienced our own vulnerability. This is the God who in Jesus Christ, the Son of God and the Son of Man, was *stretched out*—to the uttermost—on the hard wood of the cross: stretched out, broken, poured out, holding nothing back—so that we might have the peace that none other and nothing other can give. That's the God we can trust. That's the God who can handle anything. That's a God we know will never let us down, come what may.

> "Not only that, we also boast in our sufferings, knowing that suffering produces endurance, and endurance produces character, and character produces hope and hope does not disappoint us, because God's love has been poured into our hearts thorough the Holy Spirit that has been given to us." (5:3–5)

"The Merchant and the Pearl"

Year A, Proper 12: Matt 13:45–46

Sunday, July 27, 2014

From the very rich reading from Matthew's Gospel that we just heard, I would invite us to direct our attention to two of its verses. So here they are, once more:

> "Again, the Kingdom of heaven is like a merchant in search of fine pearls; on finding one pearl of great value, he went and sold all that he had and bought it."

A merchant in search of fine pearls who finds one and gives all to acquire it: for some time, I have eagerly desired to open this parable with you, and seek to hear what God—our good God—has to say to us in it, and through it.

Let's start by recollecting the teaching of A. J. Levine, who was with us just a few weeks ago at the Church of the Holy Spirit. Amy Jill Levine is a Jewish New Testament scholar, teaching at Vanderbilt University. She has done remarkable work, in particular, on the parables.[1]

I'm going to begin by noting for us some of the observations and insight she brings to bear on this very one. After that—I should hope with the Spirit's help—I'm going to invite us to take an additional step.

Dr. Levine reminded us that the parables of Jesus are not innocuous. They don't simply restate the obvious. They're often highly subversive. So the parable of the merchant in search of fine pearls tells us a good deal more than merely saying that the kingdom of heaven is valuable. Well yes, of course; this we should know already. Jesus didn't need to say a parable to

---

1. See Levine, *Short Stories by Jesus*.

say only that. The kingdom of heaven is certainly valuable and worth desiring, but Jesus is saying more. So let's bring the story back to mind.

There's this pearl merchant. He already has many pearls: lots of them. They're his *business*. He buys and sells them. But he finds one: one that he sells everything else to acquire. Now, what is he going to do with that one pearl? He can't make much of a meal of it, and as Dr. Levine said, if he'd try to wear it, it wouldn't cover very much at all, either. But he stakes everything—everything he has—to get it. Strange, isn't it?

As we live ever more deeply into the reality of God's kingdom, we are summoned—we are empowered—to ponder how we actually order our lives: how we value things. We're invited to notice in ways that maybe we never noticed before, just what it is upon which we are staking everything else. Sometimes we do so wisely, and sometimes—as we all know too well—we do so foolishly. There are times when we stake everything on something that isn't worth it, that is not, in fact, our true hearts' desire.

Life in God's kingdom calls us to ponder such realities. What is it upon which we're staking everything? Really? That can be either a hard or an enlivening question to face. Maybe both. Maybe we're afraid that we couldn't stand the answers. But this is an "enabled-in-the-kingdom" kind of question, from which we no longer need to pull back.

Wisely or foolishly, lovingly or selfishly: what is—or what have we made—"the one thing needful" (Luke 10:42 KJV), for which we will sacrifice all else?

Well worth pondering, even if not fully comfortable to do so.

Now, I'll invite us to take that additional step:

The seed of the kingdom is the good news. And the good news given to us in this teaching story, as all good news is, is a matter of *who God is—and what God is doing.* The gospel is not a matter of mere human moralizing. The gospel is not a message that says, simply, "Try harder." Or somehow conjures up within ourselves more appropriate feelings. That leads nowhere. The human project, by itself and in itself, does not lead to life.

Now, as I think many of you know, Lori and I just got back from our three weeks in Northwestern Montana early yesterday morning, and it's good to be back. Yet as we emerged from our three weeks in the Montana woods, where we didn't have TV and didn't listen to radio and didn't have access to email or internet, we again heard the news of the nation and the world. And as we hear that news, it is evident that not much has changed. More violence. More heartbreak. More manifest and injurious human

"The Merchant and the Pearl"

failure. It seems as though this world community of ours is broken up into competing utopianisms, each so self-righteously and imperviously infatuated with its own sense of right. It doesn't lead anywhere very good, does it?

So we should know, at these deepest levels, that the good news has to be much more—and the good news has to be radically different—than merely more of our human "stuff." So as we hear this little parable, let's ask how we learn of the good news in a fresh and powerful way. In it, let's look, first, for its indications of who God is and what God is doing.

In fact, in this little teaching story, the parable of the merchant in search of fine pearls, Jesus is telling us something he considers *essential* that we know about God's character and most specifically, in God's character as it was being manifested in Jesus' own ministry.

Where is God in this remarkable story?

But before trying to answer this, it may be helpful to look at its context: the stories—the parables—immediately around it. Prior to it, we have two stories concerning sowers who sow good seed (even in the face of both impediments and sabotage), then a man who planted a mustard seed, and then a woman mixing yeast into her flour. And after, we hear of the fishermen who throw their net into the sea, and when that net is full of its assorted catch, they draw it ashore. These are all stories in which Jesus is indicating what God is doing, through and in his ministry. And in the narratives of all of these, in mysterious ways, it is *the Lord himself* who is indicated as the protagonist, as the *prime act-or*.

So then, where is God in the parable of the merchant in search of fine pearls?

Suppose that it's not just another bit of pious moralizing. Suppose in this story that it is *God* who is the reckless merchant in search of fine pearls. Suppose it is God who is willing to make a reckless acquisition—foolish in the world's eyes. And if it is God who is the merchant in search of fine pearls, what then is the pearl of great price?

Well, dear ones, that would be *you*.

It is you, in the story, who are the pearl of great price—for whom God in Christ is willing to stake everything: to redeem us, to call us back to living fellowship in himself.

God's love may indeed be foolish by the world's standards. It may be reckless. But God's love is not unmindful, because God knows the utter cost of this enterprise.

> "Christ Jesus ... though he was in the form of God, did not regard equality with God as something to be exploited, but emptied himself, taking the form of a slave, being born in human likeness. And being found in human form, he humbled himself and became obedient to the point of death—even death on a cross." (Phil 2:5b-8)

So, today's text, which we may have thought was fairly innocuous, in fact points with sure indication to the utterly sacrificial love of the God we meet in Jesus. This little parable points to the expanse—indeed, the chasm—of love found in the cross of Christ. So, it is we who are the pearl of great price.[2]

Now, I don't know about you, but when I hear that message, when I try and take it into my spirit, there's a big part of me that says, "You've got to be kidding, Lord. Am I worth that? In my fallibility, in my inconstancy, in the smallness of my life?" The word of grace that we meet in Jesus says, "Yes. I meant what I said, and I mean what I am doing."

And if we can come to see ourselves in this new and astounding light—everything changes. Maybe suddenly. More often incrementally. But we can no longer see ourselves, or anybody else, in the same light. Because the others, too, are also the pearl of God's great price. Not because of anything that any of us bring to the table but because of God's own astounding and utterly gracious generosity.

This isn't mere niceness. It's the remaking of the universe.

> "Again, the kingdom of heaven is like a merchant in search of fine pearls; on finding one pearl of great value he went and sold all that he had and bought it."

---

2. This perspective on the sermon's text is not the majority view. To be sure, is generally apt to be cautious with "alternative" interpretations. These can lead to unhealthy places, evasions of—rather than real engagements with—the text. Before setting forth a different take on Bible passage, one must ask if that take coheres with its immediate context, its greater setting of the book in which it is found, and whether or not it is consistent with the analogy of faith.

Christ purchasing (or being the ransom for) his people is well attested in Scripture and carried forward, prominently, in the early church fathers. Luther's *Small Catechism* speaks of our having been "purchased and won" by Christ (pt. 2, article 2; *Lutheran Confessions*, 329).

But the understanding of this passage set forward here does not necessarily obliterate the more common interpretation. Keeping well in mind the appropriate cautions, we ought to recognize that sometimes the Scriptures can be authentically polyvalent—that is, that they may genuinely carry more than one layer or dimension of meaning. (As is the case with a number of literary genres in general.)

"The Merchant and the Pearl"

As I was pondering this message—Yes—the words of a poem came to my mind. And I was drawn specifically to one of George Herbert, the great English priest and poet. Some of us know it, I'm sure. But it's worth hearing again. The title of the poem is "Love." It's the third poem of Herbert's so titled, and I'll conclude by sharing it:

> Love bade me welcome. Yet my soul drew back
> > Guilty of dust and sin.
> But quick-eyed Love, observing me grow slack
> > From my first entrance in,
> Drew nearer to me, sweetly questioning,
> > If I lacked any thing.
>
> A guest, I answered, worthy to be here:
> > Love said, You shall be he.
> I the unkind, ungrateful? Ah my dear,
> > I cannot look on thee.
> Love took my hand, and smiling did reply,
> > Who made the eyes but I?
>
> Truth Lord, but I have marred them: let my shame
> > Go where it doth deserve.
> And know you not, says Love, who bore the blame?
> > My dear, then I will serve.
> You must sit down, says Love, and taste my meat:
> > So I did sit and eat.[3]

---

3. Herbert, *Complete English Poems*, 178.

"On This Day the Lord Has Acted"

Easter Sunday Morning, Year B: Mark 16:1–8

April 5, 2015

Alleluia! Christ is risen!

"Lord, it is good for us to be here!" (Mark 9:9)

Indeed so! But we're not here merely because we have certain ideas about Jesus. We're not here only because we like to tell stories about Jesus. We are here because Jesus—who was crucified and died—was raised from death. We are here because Jesus is alive. That's why we think about him—and why we tell the great story.

Resurrection is not a matter of *our* ideas, our storytelling, our agendas. Resurrection is not matter of mere legacy, not merely memories among those who are left behind. It also is not just some overwrought metaphor for spring coming every year, the return of green. Lilies and daffodils and such don't need to be symbolized by something else. They speak adequately enough on their own behalf, in their beauty and fragrance—and the great abundance of their pollen.

Resurrection is new and indestructible life raised from death. Christ—the Christ who was crucified, died, and was buried—is risen. And he is the enduring subject of the theological sentence. He is alive; he is acting. I can't *prove* that to you. That's not my job—although I will say that the evidence for it is compelling. But I can bid you to open hearts. Even more importantly, I can pray the Spirit of God to open *all* of our hearts here, to receive this truth of all truths, to receive it either afresh or maybe for the first time.

Jesus is not the metaphor. He's the reality. And his resurrection is the in-breaking of the most real—the most real that ever could be or ever will be. Jesus isn't the metaphor—we are. And he is drawing us ever more perfectly into his new and indestructible reality. It goes beyond death, but it starts right here, right now—and it makes the essential difference. Everything else, all our symbols, all our metaphors—and our own selves—make sense when drawn into his reality, the new grounding of our life: Jesus is alive.

This year, in the Gospel reading, we hear Mark's account of the resurrection.

> When the sabbath was over, Mary Magdalene, and Mary the mother of James, and Salome bought spices, so that they might go and anoint him. And very early on the first day of the week, when the sun had risen, they went to the tomb. They had been saying to one another, "Who will roll away the stone for us from the entrance to the tomb?" When they looked up, they saw that the stone, which was very large, had already been rolled back. As they entered the tomb, they saw a young man, dressed in a white robe, sitting on the right side; and they were alarmed. But he said to them, "Do not be alarmed; you are looking for Jesus of Nazareth, who was crucified. He has been raised; he is not here. Look, there is the place they laid him. But go, tell his disciples and Peter that he is going ahead of you to Galilee; there you will see him, just as he told you." So they went out and fled from the tomb, for terror and amazement had seized them; and they said nothing to anyone, for they were afraid.

That's it. As odd as it may seem, that's quite likely how Mark's Gospel originally ended. Strange, abrupt. Not much of an ending at all—but maybe that's the point. Maybe Mark is saying, "Now it all begins."

OK. But it still seems somewhat disquieting, doesn't it? "Amazement had seized them." I think that I get that. Of course they would be amazed. Who wouldn't be? But the part about being afraid: perhaps—at least initially—that may be harder to get our minds around. But this isn't a mere "happy ending" before the credits roll. Fear isn't only a response to bad things, the destructive and the injurious. *We can have a holy and wondrous fear in the face of an overwhelming good.*

But culturally, of late, that there seems to be no longer so much room for the concept. The spiritual preference now trends to the non-risky and non-disquieting. Of course, we can all think of certain *others* who *ought* to be disquieted. It's a different matter, though, when it comes to *us*. Presently, our immediate religious inclination (if we incline that way at all) is likely to go for it in one of its *well-tamed* forms. But today of all days, why would we settle for tamed religion?

After all, is it written,

> The fear of the LORD is the beginning of wisdom. (Ps 111:10, Prov 9:10)

Perhaps some more everyday examples—not nearly as apocalyptic: less vast, less cosmic, and much more modest—might help us begin to re-approach the concept. I'll risk offering three of these from my own life, by way of illustration. But I much hope that they might inspire you to think of how such a dynamic may have been at work in your own experience, as well.

First, from early childhood, I was drawn to music. Deeply so. At a certain point—I was eight or nine—I began to badger my parents for a violin. Then, at long last, on Christmas Day, I got it—sized just right for my age. I opened the case and saw. It was beautiful. Exquisite. The sheer excellence of it gave me a stab of joy! I was utterly delighted but also, almost in the same moment, was afraid. Truly so. Suddenly this had become serious. This was going to change who I was. This was going to mean *lessons*. It was going to mean a *lot* of practice. And I knew very well that the sounds that I would produce would be nothing at all like Isaac Stern!

Another example, one that I've shared with you before: since my family's first visit there in 1996, Glacier National Park has been, for me, what I must call a sacred place. (And I don't use that characterization lightly.) Its "Going to the Sun Highway" takes one over the top of a glacier-sculpted high pass. Memory can never hold—and photos can never capture—the grandeur. The views one gets on that drive reframe all things. I love it so. "O LORD, how manifold are thy works! In wisdom hast thou made them all" (Ps 104:24 RSV). Yet I have a real issue with heights. So along with the delight, I also experience some genuine distress. At least for the time being, I can't have one without the other.

Lastly, I remember my courtship with Lori. (And, of course, I'm sharing this with her permission!) For a while, we had been music majors together in college. At a certain point, the possibility of a significant relationship increasingly began to emerge. But the problem was that I was then already on track to go to seminary—at a school all the way across the country. So I was in a quandary. But as the line from Jurassic Park says, "Life finds a way." And on Easter Sunday, 1976, I invited her to an afternoon dinner party that

"On This Day the Lord Has Acted"

I was throwing for my friends. When dinner was over, I drove her home. As we were saying goodbye, the prospect of a kiss presented itself—and it was certainly a desirable prospect. But I knew that this would be no casual thing. It would be a kiss that would change the world. My tightly-figured-out life plan would now become uncertain. My preferred mindset of "it's all set, I'm in control, and there are no variables" would have to go. There was some risk in being open to that moment and I knew it.

Perhaps these—such as they are—might serve to illustrate the concept: fearful things don't necessarily have to be bad!

So maybe we *can* begin to understand why the women who heard the first resurrection message were afraid. Maybe we'd be more afraid, too, if we really heard that message more deeply.

But our text also says that the women at the tomb were *terrified*.

> So they went out and fled from the tomb, for terror and amazement had seized them. (16:8)

This is even harder to get our minds around than fear. The word "terror," in our modern setting, brings images of the intentionally destructive, the intentionally brutal, to mind. All that which is terrifying radically disrupts that which had known before. And if it's intentionally terrifying, harder yet to bear. We don't like our lives messed with. We don't like our sense of stability compromised.

But—again—we're not only "threatened" by the evil and the brutal and the destructive. The in-breaking of life—new life, redefining life, the in-breaking of Truth, the in-breaking of Justice, the in-breaking of ultimate Beauty—this also threatens the life that we had known before.

But God does not disrupt our prior existence, the status quo to which we had grown accustomed, merely to make us feel bad. God breaks in in order to reclaim us and once again, to share himself, with us, in abundance. We're not talking about a "pat on the back." We're talking about life from death, beginning right now in the crucified and risen Jesus. Beginning right now—and welling up to eternity.

> "Do not be alarmed; you are looking for Jesus of Nazareth, who was crucified. He has been raised; he is not here. Look, there is the place they laid him." (16:6)

On this day the LORD has acted; we will rejoice and be glad in it. (Ps 118:24; *Book of Common Prayer*, 162)

The believing life is risky business. It's certainly a life in which we have to relinquish our notions of control. We will feel overwhelmed and maybe even threatened, sometimes, by the in-breaking of indestructible life, ultimate beauty, and truth in Jesus. But to the extent that we have begun to know him—to the extent that we are beginning to love and cherish our risen Christ—we wouldn't have it any other way.

Alleluia! Christ is risen!

"No Cross Is So Extreme, as to Have None"

Year B, Proper 19: Mark 8:27–38

Sunday, September 13, 2015

YESTERDAY MORNING, AT ABOUT one in the morning, Lori and I returned from our three weeks in the Montana mountains—but it's good to be back here in this place, to see all your faces; it's good to be back with you as we gather in the Lord's service.

The doctrine of the cross is right at the heart of Christian faith. Yet we hear voices these days saying it's too difficult, too offensive. Maybe we need to move on. But we *can't* "move on" from the cross and remain who and what we are in Jesus. In response to such voices, I'm inclined to ask: Is it only now we discover that the doctrine of the cross is difficult? This shouldn't have been a surprise; it's been clear from the very beginning. Didn't Paul underscore that the cross is foolishness and scandal? (1 Cor 1:18–23). Jesus himself made clear from the beginning both the centrality and difficulty of the cross. We hear about that in today's gospel.

Right in the middle of Mark's Gospel, right at the pivot of the narrative, Jesus led his disciples to take the next step of knowing who he is and what he is doing. He opened up a conversation: "Those folks out there, who do they say that I am?" They gave various answers, then Jesus asked, pointedly,

> "But who do *you* say that I am?" Peter answered him, "You are the Messiah," and he sternly ordered them not to tell anyone about him. (8:29–30)

This seems a perplexing instruction, doesn't it?—but critical, because without understanding the cross, neither the people "out there" nor the disciples themselves will be able to understand what Jesus means, what he intends, as Messiah.

> Then he began to teach them that the Son of Man must undergo great suffering and be rejected by the elders the chief priests and the scribes and be killed and after three days rise again. (8:31)

Peter hit the panic button—and took Jesus aside. "No! Absolutely not! Things have been going so well. Why mess it up?" Jesus rebuked Peter strongly, telling him and the rest of the disciples (including us) that he was going to the cross on purpose and of necessity. This is where everything up until now had been pointing all along.

Jesus was going to the cross to embrace the full extent of our vulnerability: to experience the worst of injustice, to take upon himself the full crisis of the human condition—and the full measure of our culpability. And there—in his utterly apparent defeat—he accomplished the victory of God: the instrument of our salvation, yours and mine—our liberation. There's no other way. There's no detour. There's no cheaper option.

Jesus called the crowd with his disciples and said to them:

> "If any want to become my followers, let them deny themselves and take up their Cross and follow me. For those who want to save their live will lose it and those who lose their live for my sake and for the sake of the gospel will save it." (8:34b-35)

When Jesus tells us that if *any* wish to become his followers they must take up their cross and follow him, he's not referring to merely putting up with life's frustrations. Nor can it be reduced to a challenge to some "percentage" (in which we ourselves are not included) who really have it coming.

"If *any*." That's a 100 percent proposition. Our Lord's saying is a summons—to all and to each, no matter what our condition—to be bound up with him on the cross and in the sacrificial way of the cross.

In our baptism we are united with the death of Christ (Rom 6:3). And every Sunday, when we gather in Eucharist, when we break the bread and share the cup, we "proclaim the Lord's death until he comes" (1 Cor 11:26). So, even if we are far too forgetful of it, we *are* now bound up with the crucified Jesus—bound up with his cross and the terrible, wonderful victory he accomplished there.

How could we ever expect that things thereafter would be "the same"? A new way of being, a different kind of life: We are to live, we are to think,

"No Cross Is So Extreme, as to Have None"

relate, and we are to act—in a cross-shaped manner. Our lives, our action, our thinking, are to be *cruciform*. The words of Paul in his letter to the Galatians come to mind.

> I have been crucified with Christ; and it is no longer I who live, but it is Christ who lives in me. And the life I now live in the flesh I live by faith in the Son of God, who loved me and gave himself up for me . . . May I never boast of anything else except the Cross of our Lord Jesus Christ, by which the world has been crucified to me, and I to the world. (2:20, 6:14)

Christians, by definition then, aren't a people who just fit into the stuff that's going on around us: we are to be different on the inside and different on the outside.

So, how do we live more fully into the cruciform life in the here and now? I'm thinking a lot about that as we are head into yet another national election cycle—with the "big day" a year and a couple of months from now. I almost don't know anybody—except political or media professionals—who's getting a charge from this process. Yes, when the time comes, I'll probably do my civic duty and vote, but I'm weary of the business already and don't expect it to get better. How about you? It's my own considered sense that this coming cycle could be among the most polarizing and toxic of all national elections in United States history.

What are we to do, then—and *be*—as Christ's people in this context?

You know how it is when I go to the woods; the poetry starts to percolate up. Even more than usual. Well, there's one poem of late that's been speaking to me of our current condition—although it's the better part of a century old. W. B. Yeats. Here's the just the first stanza of his poem "The Second Coming":

> Turning and turning in the widening gyre
> The falcon cannot hear the falconer;
> Things fall apart; the centre cannot hold;
> Mere anarchy is loosed upon the world,
> The blood-dimmed tide is loosed, and everywhere
> The ceremony of innocence is drowned;
> The best lack all conviction, while the worst
> Are full of passionate intensity.[1]

---

1. Yeats, *Collected Poems*, 187.

In such a context, it can be very tempting for churches just to go along: do business the way business is done. The various political partisanships divide up the American denominational spoils. Why not accept the assignment of being cheerleaders to one institutionally preferred ideological team or another?

But this surely doesn't sound like what Jesus had in mind! To fold in words of another poet, how could Jesus have been satisfied with his people serving as cheerleaders—really, superfluous cheerleaders—to the "ignorant armies clashing by night"?[2]

We are to be exemplars of a different way of living—a different way of *being*. Maybe what would be of some *real* benefit to this present world would be more folks who had a keener sense of their *heavenly* citizenship. Maybe it would be for the actual betterment of our society—our deeply divided, polarized society—if we had a few more people who could lay their passions, political and otherwise, down before the passion of Christ.

I'm not saying that we ought to be apathetic, disengaged people, but we are to be transformed. The church needs to very clear about this, I believe, lest we be co-opted. And I don't believe Jesus sent us into the world to be co-opted: to give insipid versions of what can already be readily obtained elsewhere. The issues of the day have their importance, full of social and moral significance. We will certainly hear about them out there unendingly, in huge doses.

We've heard the old complaint about those who are "so heavenly minded that they're of no earthly good." There was something to that, of course. Yet I sense, in our own context, that the more active risk is that we're of so little earthly good precisely because we're too exclusively earthly minded. The solution to the world's crisis is not that the world acquire more of itself. (If that's really possible.) We need Something Else.

Here, in the ministry of Christian preaching, we have ten minutes a week. Well, sometimes in my own case, maybe a little more than ten minutes! I have, more and more, a keen sense of the urgency—the urgency and the very present relevance—of eternity. For anyone here, right now, this might be our last Sunday; this might be the last sermon. For any of us, the question posed by poet and preacher John Donne is both pointed and apt: "What if this present were the world's last night?"[3]

---

2. Arnold, "Dover Beach," 86.
3. "The Cross," in Donne, *Complete English Poems*, 326.

"No Cross Is So Extreme, as to Have None"

"What the world needs now" is not sentimentalism but the capacity of perceiving the real; specifically, *under the aspect of eternity*. The gospel proclamation is this: we only get to such perception—such an illumination—through the darkness of the cross.

Different clergy have different approaches. Blessings be. It's not that I'm unaware of other options. My own is deliberate, well-considered, proceeds out of conviction—and is bound up with my own particular sense of call.

For example: if I say nothing about "climate change" in my preaching time—absolutely nothing—for the next year, I'm still fully confident that you will hear of it from many sources—and in highly substantial measure. (And this may be entirely apt.) However, I have very little confidence that the world "out there" will proclaim the gospel to you in my stead.

We are to be the bearers, in Christ and by Christ, of an eternal way of being. It has broken through to us by the cross. So, how do we get our minds and our hearts and our spirits more cross-shaped—more cruciform? After all, this could be much more the way to affect real change in our broken world than we ever suspected. Why then this confidence in loading ourselves up with that with which the world is already stuffed?

I'm not saying that in preaching we never address a contemporary issue. We may, and indeed, sometimes we must—in obedience to the word of God. But please be aware, when we think we want the preacher to "speak out" on this or that or the other: after the fact, if the preacher did so, we might end up wishing we hadn't gotten our desires granted. Frankly, some of the time, I wonder if the call for "prophetic preaching" is actually a desire to be congratulated for our very fine sociopolitical sensibilities.

The eternal—revealed under the aspect of the cross—is always a good deal more contemporary than we think. And the people formed therein is an instrument God is using by which he is "making all things new" (Rev 21:5).

So, in my own ministry, I am less interested in telling people *what* to think, about this or that or the other but rather much more concerned with *how* we think—from the core, from the heart—as Christians.

Because wherever we come down on our individual politics and however we might line up on this or that cluster of issues, our mission, our purpose—the reason we're here, why we're taking up a bit of the earth—is that we are a people claimed, and now being transformed, specifically through the cross of Jesus. Hearts have to die with Christ and live with him again. Everything flows from there: all that we will then do and be. No other way.

Will we lay our passions down before the passion of Christ?

> Jesus said, "If any want to become my followers, let them deny themselves and take up their Cross and follow me. For those who want to save their live will lose it and those who lose their live for my sake and for the sake of the gospel will save it." (Mark 8:34b-35)

Jesus must go to the cross, his journey must go there; so must we. But the journey doesn't end there: neither his nor ours. Because this indispensable cross, around which there is no faithful detour, is the gate to resurrection. Praise be.

To conclude, it seems apt to return—again—to poetry; once more from John Donne:

> SINCE Christ embraced the cross itself, dare I
> His image, th' image of His cross, deny?
> Would I have profit by the sacrifice,
> And dare the chosen altar to despise?
> It bore all other sins, but is it fit
> That it should bear the sin of scorning it? . . .
>
> From me no pulpit, nor misgrounded law,
> Nor scandal taken, shall this cross withdraw,
> It shall not, for it cannot; for the loss
> Of this cross were to me another cross.
> Better were worse, for no affliction,
> No cross is so extreme, as to have none.

"Love Bears All Things"

Fourth Sunday after Epiphany, Year A: 1 Cor 13:1–13 and Luke 4:22–30

Sunday, January 31, 2016

THE GOSPEL READING THAT we just heard contains such a shocking, truly disturbing, shift in the attitude of the people to Jesus. They started off very pleased but didn't stay that way for very long. "All spoke well of him," but only a little later, "all . . . were filled with rage. They got up, [and] drove him out of the town" (Luke 4:22, 28–29a).

Among the many lessons we might draw from this is the clarity that not even Jesus made everybody happy. If the sign of our authentic faith, if the sign of our real spirituality, is that we "make" everybody happy, we have to ask, hearing today's gospel passage: what about Jesus? If *that* was the enterprise, he certainly was a spectacular failure.

So, at the least: if the Son of God doesn't "make" everybody happy, it's unlikely that God expects *us* to try to "make" everybody happy—nor should we have that expectation of others. The truth is, we cannot "make" *anybody* happy, including *ourselves*. (All we can do in regard to our own happiness—and this only with God's help—is to cultivate the disposition, and the habits, that make happiness an increasing likelihood.)

This leads to our principal focus this morning. I would invite us to draw our attention to today's second Scripture lesson, from Paul's First Letter to the Corinthians: chapter thirteen—the love chapter. Even people who have characteristically a problem with Paul often are able easily to delight in First Corinthians Thirteen. It's not for nothing that this wonderful passage is often chosen to be read at weddings.

> If I speak in the tongues of mortals and of angels, but do not have love, I am a noisy gong or a clanging cymbal. And if I have prophetic powers, and understand all mysteries and all knowledge, and if I have all faith, so as to remove mountains, but do not have love, I am nothing. If I give away all my possessions, and if I hand over my body so that I may boast, but do not have love, I gain nothing. (13:1–3)

So, once again; I'm going to invite us to lean in.

Nevertheless, there may be one element—so obvious that we may miss it—that we must consider if we're to understand this passage, so that we may truly take it to heart. Paul—or the Spirit of God through Paul—is saying a lot of things here about love. But what, in the first place, do we *mean* by the word "love"? More importantly, what might the Holy Spirit mean by it, in this great and so well-known chapter?

Fact is, in this human condition of ours, we're often rather confused about what love really is—and about what love isn't. And I don't think the church is immune from this confusion. Not by a long shot. To the point, I believe that there's a particular confusion about this—what love is and what love isn't—which is one of the greatest threats in the contemporary church to the vitality of our future mission. This is the confusion of codependency for love.

Now, this is going to take some unpacking—and will engage us in some difficult work.

"Codependency" is a term that often comes up in contexts of addiction or abuse. Given what our lives are, I'm fully aware that we likely have many gathered here this morning who have dealt with abusive or addictive situations—and maybe both. So this is risky territory, a topic that may have a good deal more immediate relevance to our personal lives than we may be comfortable acknowledging. And I'll have challenges to our thinking that I'll be inviting us to consider—all of us.

So, calling on God's leading—God's strength, God's truth, God's mercy—let's lean in.

Codependency is a learned behavior; actually, it's a *survival mechanism* in seriously compromised situations. Furthermore, it's *much* easier to learn personally, where it's already taken root in our environment. It's catching: in fact, highly infectious. Having said this, it's important to underscore that people often first learn codependency when they're in positions of great vulnerability—trying to do the best they can at the time in dangerous, high-stakes settings. This needs to be acknowledged with great compassion. The problem is that this survival mechanism, as understandable as it may have been at the time, is one that cannot serve people well as they go forward. It can become a habitual, even predominant, life-disposition that can inflict its own considerable injury on others and on our own selves.

Codependency doesn't only operate in family systems. It can take root, as well, in cultures, in organizations—and most certainly, I would stress, in the church.

So, before we go on, what are we talking about here? I've put together a working definition, for our purposes this morning, especially as significant for church relational systems. There's a lot in it, to be sure; perhaps much that we'll need to continue to think about in the time to come.

Here it is, and I've printed this definition out on the bottom of the inside cover of the bulletin, if you wish to follow along.

> CODEPENDENCY—A WORKING DEFINITION: Codependency is a minimizing, enabling response to chronically abusive/boundary-violating behavior. Although frequently cloaked in the language of love, codependency is in fact profoundly self-centered. It procures "benefits" (of various sorts) for the codependent, usually at the greater expense of others, and is counter to the actual better interests of the person caught in the abusive pattern of behavior.

Now this topic, the confusion of codependency for love, is one that I preach about this morning with some considerable trepidation. Certainly with much thought and self-question. Once again: this is risky territory. But I am convinced that it is my obligation as your preacher to do so.

If we are to hear First Corinthians Thirteen as the living word of God that it is, we must have the right idea about what love is—and what it *isn't*. If we're confused about what the word "love" really signifies, this beautiful chapter might not only lose its meaning. Its meaning might get corrupted to something rather ungodly, twisted to say something it never could say—and never meant to say.

Before we go on though, let's highlight a critically important qualifier. When we are speaking of "codependency," we're speaking of an unhealthy response to *chronically abusive, boundary violating, and seriously disruptive behavior*. We are *not* talking about the everyday quandaries, the natural frustrations of knowing how to deal with ourselves and one another, sinners that we are. Codependency, rather, is a particular response to specific acute situations.

We are, *all of us*, from time to time at least, both difficult and disappointing. That's not what we're talking about here. In response to the inevitable disagreeability we experience in one another from time to time, we are, indeed, as Paul puts it in the Letter to the Galatians, to "bear one another's burdens, and in this way . . . fulfil the law of Christ" (6:2).

On the other hand, the specific confusion we're considering—codependency for love—is a response to chronically abusive or boundary-violating behavior that is *unhealthy* and actually *unloving*. And it procures "benefits." Yes, it does. We get something unholy out of the codependent deal.

I know that this is can be a very hard truth to face—and at least to some degree, we *all* deal with it. Realizing that codependency is not altruism can be one of the hardest, but still necessary, steps that we have to take in our spiritual growth.

Well, what might some ungodly benefits of codependency be?

Here's one: we get to avoid the hot seat—or at least the *hotter* seat. Put more simply, conflict avoidance. We keep ourselves in a position of comparative safety. The greater price of the situation gets passed on to someone else.

Here's another: we get to keep thinking of ourselves as the "nice" ones, the "kind" ones. Someone else will have to be the heavy. And it can be made to sound very devout as well. Lots of pious stuff has been quoted to injured people from positions of relative advantage.

And yet another common benefit of codependency is that we get to preserve the circumstances of our life the way we like them: not too disrupted.

None of these sounds like truly loving behavior, do they?

Codependency is, in fact, profoundly self-centered. (Remember, it starts off as a personal survival mechanism.) It does *not* serve the better interests of others, including the person with the identified troubles. (Truth is, it doesn't even address our own best interests either, but the point at hand is getting past the habit of confusing it for love.)

And love, the real thing—Love, capital L; the Love we hear about in First Corinthians Thirteen—is *other directed*. True love is directed toward the actual wellbeing of the other.

"Love Bears All Things"

This is the case not only for individuals—but also for persons in community. Nowhere more so than the community of faith. I'm convinced that systemic, habitualized codependency is one of the greatest threats to the church's well-being. For examples one doesn't have to look far.

Many of us in recent weeks have seen the movie *Spotlight*—a powerful and very difficult-to-watch portrayal of the cover-up of the sexual abuse of children, on a huge scale, in the Boston Archdiocese. Other expressions of codependent culture in the church—much more subtle, nowhere near as horrific but still widespread and destructive—abound. In congregation after congregation, enabling, minimizing responses to acting out, and bullying behavior cause real injury, not to mention a colossal waste of the church's life energy.

We were sent into the world as bearers of God's love in Christ—Holy Love—not to be serving ourselves in the phony gospel of niceness: the real thing, not the counterfeit. If all this sounds discouraging, it certainly is. But we must remember that God's great work of regeneration, only later to be recognized for what it was, often *begins* in us with our sense of discouragement, our sense of conviction and burden.

The old song says:

> You've got to walk that lonesome valley,
> You've got to go by yourself.
> Nobody else going to go there for you;
> You've got to go there by yourself.

Yes, that's what it feels like, truly so. That's what it *must* feel like, at a critical point. We've got to get going, and we don't know how. However, thanks be: later down the road—perhaps much later—we make the retroactive discovery of grace: the grace that had been there all along. We were *never* really alone; we were never traveling by our own strength. There's only One who took that journey by himself. He did so we wouldn't have to.

But—of course—are we not to discount the terrible sense of God's absence through which we must sometimes pass through. But when what God gives is a sense of his absence, how infinitely more valuable is *that* than any replacements with which we would desperately use to try to fill the space. Nevertheless, ultimately, by grace, even if it be far after the fact, we will come to recognize the presence, then, of the One who had given himself to us, for a time, in unrecognition and hiddenness.

All this business with which we've been wrestling; it's *hard* stuff. We think about our personal stories—the relationships and communities we're involved in and on which we depend. The questions and answers here are seldom simple. We can't always count on ready-to-go scripts that can easily or quickly tell us just how much is codependency and how much is real love in the complicated, often contradictory mix of our blended lives. And even when we begin to come to some hard-won clarities, there usually aren't ready-to-go scripts or simple answers for what to *do* about it. This is hard stuff. Nevertheless, engaging it is a part of living into the healing and recovery that God has in store for all of us.

We won't get it completely right all at once. The point is doing the work that God is giving us to do: keeping at it, relying on God's grace every step of the way, bearing with the challenges of a long process—and often walking in uncertainty. That sounds pretty loving, doesn't it? A loving born of God's love, the real thing.

I'll share a key distinction that may be of substantial ongoing help as we sort things out—if we consider it deeply and well. Let's go again to First Corinthians Thirteen: "[Love] bears all things . . . endures all things" (13:7). That's what it says. Indeed so. However, the text does *not* say, "Love has *other* people bear all things; love has *other* people endure all things."

That's a critical difference, isn't it?

"Bearing all things" *ourselves* might include such things as accepting the fact that we can't "make" everyone happy. It might involve confronting our own addiction to approval or acknowledging our deep-seated tendencies to play it safe—evade risk—when others are counting on us, when coming through for them would put us out of our comfort zone.

"Bearing all things" may mean taking a painful look at the benefits—or "cuts"—that we may be getting from the codependent deal when so much in us instead just wants to keep telling ourselves how "nice" or "friendly" we are.

Finally, "bearing all things" sometimes will require naming boundaries with those who don't want to hear them named—and then accepting the consequences of having done so.

In other words, real love puts itself on the hot seat.

The godly love we hear about in First Corinthians Thirteen builds up our soul (both personal and corporate); it bears us, more and more surely, in the river of eternal life. The phony substitutes corrode us from the inside—and end in death.

Pretty heavy stuff. Yes, it is. We may well ask: Where's the good news? Where's the gospel? Where's the word from heaven?

"Love Bears All Things"

Here it is: *God has not been codependent with us*—even though we once thought that's what we wanted. Our agenda was non-disruption. We may have wanted blessings of sorts but certainly not interference. Instead, God has given us what we *needed*. God has been truly loving, "for God is love" (1 John 4:8b)—righteous, compassionate, transformative, other-directed, "for us and for our salvation." Good news: God was willing to put his own self right on the ultimately costly hot seat to do so.

That's what—and that's who—we meet in Jesus, who bore the full cost of dealing with the likes of us, in *love*. The real thing. In the Lord Jesus Christ—"and him crucified" (1 Cor 2:2)—we know, at long last, what love is.

For those in Christ, it is no more a *truly* lonesome passage (even if might sometimes feel that way), but it may be a long one. It'll be OK. To be sure, our motives—even our best intentions—are never absolutely "pure." Not at this present stage of the journey. We are now, all of us, still sinners in a sinful world. We aren't to drive ourselves to distraction with the anxious insistence on immediate perfection. (Such an insistence is just another form of self-centeredness.)

The critical matter is not our own scrupulosity but rather this: God's great work of salvation. Are we living into it? Is it becoming more and more characteristic of us? Are we growing up in Christ, growing into *his* Love? (Eph 4:13). The point isn't shortcut answers but new creation! (Gal 6:15b).

> "For we know only in part, and we prophesy only in part; but when the complete comes, the partial will come to an end. When I was a child, I spoke like a child, I thought like a child, I reasoned like a child; when I became an adult, I put an end to childish ways. For now we see in a mirror, dimly, but then we will see face to face. Now I know only in part; then I will know fully, even as I have been fully known. And now faith, hope, and love abide, these three; and the greatest of these ... is *love*." (13:9–13)

"Christ Became a Curse for Us"

Sunday of the Passion, Palm Sunday: Luke 22:14—23:56 and Gal 3:13

March 20, 2016

THIS PRESENT SERVICE IS among the longest and most demanding in the entire worship year. The whole course of our Lenten journey so far is meant to bring us to a place where we may attend today with spiritual endurance, with focus of mind and heart.

We've just been propelled, uncomfortably and with great spiritual force, into Holy Week.

We began this morning with such joyful acclamation: Jesus is our true and rightful King. Then suddenly: the psalm, the passion narrative. The acclamations fade so quickly—the voices of rejection prevail. It's a difficult shift to hear—and it's on purpose.

We all want to feel that had we been there *then*, our responses would have been so different. If we had, maybe we wouldn't have gotten so scared like the brash Peter and denied his Lord in a moment of panic. If we had, surely *we* wouldn't have decided that Jesus was just too dangerous to keep around.

And certainly had we been there back then, we wouldn't have said, "Away with him!"

Surely not *we*. "Surely not I, Lord" (Matt 26:22).

But we *were* there. That "then" holds and confronts all our "nows." We are *implicated* in that "then"—even in our respectability and highest aspirations. At the least, we like to think that we maintained our pious neutrality, that we didn't "take sides." But "not choosing" is usually, in fact, making a choice—just not admitted, to ourselves or others. In our sinful humanness we *did* choose, a choice that we have recapitulated in different forms, both personal and corporate, many times, over and over again. The cross of Christ is itself the revelation of God's perfect, holy, entirely just, and final judgement. We don't need to wait until the end of time to hear the word that is impossible for us to bear.

This is not *all* that we can say today, thanks be, but it *is* part of what we must say.

Even those who have come to faith in our Savior—and rightly acclaim and receive him—now live in a presently mixed reality. There are parts in us, still all-too deep-rooted—where we're not yet responding in faith. We, too—often before we know it—get afraid at the risks of sticking with Christ; we panic, we deny, or maybe even say some new, subtle version of "away with him; away with him!" (Luke 23:18; John 19:19).

All of us, including the human Jesus, have some essential needs, which we look to our community of fellow humans to fulfil: basic safety, purpose, and perhaps most of all, a sense of real belonging. These are deep-seated, "hard-wired" needs. And yet Jesus, as he went to the cross, was stripped of *all* of them.

Well, it certainly wasn't safe going to Golgotha. It was the ultimate un-safety.

As far as purpose, to all earthly appearances, including those closest to him, Jesus would have ended his life as a *failure*. And we remember his own personal cry of abandonment on the cross: "My God, my God, why have you forsaken me?" (Matt 27:46, Mark 15:43; see Ps 22:1).

So, the deepest core human need—belonging—this, too, was stripped away from the Crucified.

Nevertheless, Jesus said, "And I, when I am lifted up from the earth, will draw all people to myself" (John 12:32).

From the place of the cross, and *to* this place, Christ calls us. What's going on here that could possibly be "good"?

A difficult verse from Paul's Letter to Galatians comes to mind, and to it, I invite us to draw our attention. Galatians, chapter 3, verse 13:

> "Christ redeemed us from the curse of the law by becoming a curse for us. For it is written, cursed is everyone who hangs on a tree."

That verse contains a citation from Deuteronomy (21:23), which says that someone executed by hanging was considered cursed and had to be buried quickly—so as not to defile the holy dwelling of God's people.

But what can it mean that *Christ* became a curse for us? Well, what do *we* do when we curse somebody? We cast them out from our hearts, into the realm of our ill will. We do this, so sadly, far too casually, and far too frequently. Perhaps we try to take it back later, but at the time, what's going on when we curse—either in words or attitude—is that we eject someone from the sphere of our positive regard. At least temporarily, *they become for us an outsider. Someone who doesn't matter.*

The Roman technique of capital punishment that we call "crucifixion" was designed to strip away *everything* from the condemned person—and do so permanently. It was the most degrading form of capital punishment that the Romans used: meant not only to torture and kill but to *dehumanize*. Victims of crucifixion would become an object of horror, even to those who loved them—and certainly also to themselves. Ejected from belonging. Ejected from recognizable humanness.[1]

Jesus was executed "outside the city gate"—outside the holy place of God's dwelling. Utterly rejected. Cast out beyond the bounds of the safe, the pious, the lovely, the respectable. *You don't belong and you don't count.* Jesus died as the ultimate outsider.

But precisely "out there," *God acted* to turn things upside-down and inside-out. "Christ redeemed us . . . by becoming a curse for us." The place of utter desolation—a "no-where," on the fringe of nothingness—becomes the new center of all things. The unpayable debt is paid; the unforgivable, forgiven. The impossible to bear, borne on our behalf, by the only One who could do so. The unbridgeable gap is now spanned.

And Jesus calls us to himself, right where he made it so. Who will trust him and heed his call? Will *you*?

Jesus speaks to all and each of us: "Come unto me all you who labor and our heavily burdened and I will give you rest" (Matt 11:28).

Jesus said that he would draw all the world to himself. The new place of that holy drawing, the place to which we are summoned, is *Calvary*. So, we can't get to Jesus by staying inside our present, comfortable insider-zones: with the hedged bets, with the not fully given new loyalty, with all our evasions and the equivocations. If we're going to respond to the call—if we're going to get to the One who is calling, we go to the cross. No other way. No "at a distance" option.

He offers rest, not evasion.

---

1. For an especially valuable exposition of the specifically dehumanizing character of crucifixion as a form of capital punishment, see Rutledge, *Crucifixion*, 72–105.

"Christ Became a Curse for Us"

In the Letter to the Hebrews, we are told:

> "Jesus suffered outside the city gate in order to sanctify the people by his own blood. Let us then go to him outside the camp and bear the abuse he endured for here we have no lasting city but we are looking for the city that is to come." (13:12–13)

"Let us then go to him," outside the bounds of all our spiritually hedged bets, and find in him the new belonging that wells up to eternal life, *starting right now*.

With the eyes of faith, we see that the cross was not a defeat but the victory of God. There's more of that victory to come—to be sure—but on Calvary, it's already begun. God restored our own humanness through the One from whom everything was taken. Jesus gave it away so we could get it back.

In him, we now belong. We have a reason to be here, and we are held in perfect care. Now, that doesn't mean it's always easy. Of course, it won't be. This present life is often difficult: unsafe, uncertain; alienating. The fact is that the sinful human condition, as it is, cannot provide what we need, not ultimately, and most deeply. And we will likely be *especially* disappointed if we look at "systems and structures" (even the most pious) to provide us what can only come from above. But through the Crucified, we have something new and indestructible in our hearts. We know, through him, that we have a belonging, a purpose and a care that nothing can destroy, no matter what. No matter what! And in him, in spite of all else, we are being drawn to a more perfect love and faith.

Jesus had to walk his lonesome journey alone, so that none of the rest of us would ever have to be. In the passion narrative we heard today, as the rejection of Christ overwhelmed everything else, there's the line "and their voices prevailed" (23:23).

So now, which voices will prevail? We think about the state of this world, about the state of our country, right now in this election cycle. We think about our contradictory lives, all the complicated stuff that's going on inside of us. Before the face of Christ, and him crucified, which voices will prevail?

But the seeming silence of God, at Calvary, speaks more effectively than all else.

More deeply, more truly, more terribly, more wonderfully: whose voice really *has* prevailed?

"Grant Us, O Lord, to Trust in You with All Our Hearts"[1]

Lectionary Year B, Proper 18: Mark 7:24–37

Sunday, September 9, 2018

"Grant us, O Lord, to trust in you with all our hearts."[2] So begins today's collect: an especially apt prayer, given the Gospel reading we just heard.

This story, of Jesus' encounter with the Syrophoenician woman—with its parallel in Matthew's Gospel (15:21–28)—has to be one of the most difficult and off-putting episodes in all the Gospels.

If it were possible to push a button and make this passage "go away," many of us might be very tempted. Jesus rebuffs, with harsh language, a mother's urgent plea to help her daughter. He relents, to be sure. But how we get there is hard to bear. It is difficult to trust when things aren't making sense, isn't it?

So, what's really going on in this most challenging of passages? This is not an easy question. But I'm seriously concerned about an increasingly popular explanation of this passage in sermons these days. This now-all-too-popular "explanation" is based on a misleading and out-of-context interpretation. And this isn't a matter of minutiae but rather, most regrettably, gets in the way of receiving the gifts God intends that we receive through this Gospel text. More specifics about this in just a bit.

In *any* writing, including the Bible, context is essential. It won't do to take a small portion, by itself, reading into it our own biases and interests,

---

1. A resource that I found especially helpful, not only in confirming but also in further expanding my sense of Mark 7:24–37 within its context is Kelly Iverson's *Gentiles in the Gospel of Mark*.

2. *Book of Common Prayer*, 233.

"Grant Us, O Lord, to Trust in You with All Our Hearts"

and then say, "That's what it's about!" With anything *except* the Bible, such a thing is evidently off-target.

A number of folks here are likely familiar with the writer Joseph Conrad. One of my favorite authors! Perhaps his best known and greatest work is his novella *Heart of Darkness*. Well, suppose that we took a few stray lines from *Heart of Darkness* and then told ourselves that what it was "really" about was—the delightful pleasures of taking a riverboat cruise?

Absurd! Obviously so.

In any writing, including the Bible, we have to take account of the context, and also the direction, of the whole.

Now, to that unfortunate but increasingly all-too-popular interpretation of Mark's story of the Syrophoenician woman. I'm naming it, now, both for the purpose of spiritual *inoculation* and also so that we can then move on to something both more accurate and genuinely life-giving.

So, here it is, as it might be summarized: Jesus was either unclear or confused about his mission, and the women here boldly challenges him, so that it becomes in effect a teaching moment—perhaps even a conversion—*for Jesus himself.* Then, having been so taught (or converted), Jesus is no longer unclear (or confused).

We'll let go, for the time being, that such an explanation is utterly unheard of in *any* of Christianity's historic streams in the past almost two thousand years. It only pops up in the last few decades. That doesn't bother us too much, though, because we're pretty comfortable with thinking that we know better, about *everything*, than everyone who has come before us.

But my point, today, is that this way of understanding the text is *impossible*, once we take a look beyond these few verses by themselves—once we read the passage in the context of Mark's Gospel, as a whole.

Read as a whole, it's beyond evident that Mark *never* intends to present Jesus as unclear (or confused) about what he was doing. Mark *never* gives us a Jesus who needs to be brought to a "next stage" of his personal evolution. And Mark *never* presents other people as knowing more than Jesus, as needing to teach or challenge him, in order to bring him, somehow, "up to his potential."

This may be a "Jesus" that we would prefer (sometimes), but it's not the Jesus that the text gives us. Not remotely.

What's really going on with this? What's going on with *us*, that we would get a charge from a way of hearing this text (or *any* text) that puts *us* in the position of knowing more than Jesus knew—of being more "evolved" than he was?

Nothing very healthy at all, to say the least. I can't imagine anything farther from the intention of the Gospel writers—any of them—than to inspire such an attitude in anyone, including us.

Rather, the Gospel writers were clear that it was their job, then, to give us the Jesus we *need*—not the ones we think we might prefer. And the church today has—through them—that very same task.

So, let's proceed—let's pull the camera back—and take a look at today's difficult passage in its broader context.

Mark's Gospel begins abruptly, covering in very few verses John the Baptist's appearance, the baptism of Jesus, and his temptation in the wilderness before launching into the Galilean ministry. Galilee was Jewish territory—and our Lord's home region. It's the site of the first major section of Mark. The concluding section of the Gospel takes place, of course, in Jerusalem—*geographically* speaking, the spiritual center of Jewish life and identity. Both in Galilee and in Jerusalem, Jesus faced increasing opposition—official opposition from his own tradition's religious authorities. This will lead to his rejection and death.

But there's an *in-between* section—in between Jerusalem and the initial, exclusively Galilean ministry. This is when, in Mark's story line, our Lord makes a series of what we might call incursions—from Galilee, into other regions, distinctly non-Jewish: in other words, gentile territory. If we track these travels on a map, they might at first look like detours. This is not the case! They're deliberate departures from "home"; they are *purposeful incursions* of Jesus into the outside world—the specifically pagan world—before he heads to the cross. That this is no accident is made clear by Mark's Gospel itself, which is very evidently written for a gentile audience.

By the way, the trip to Tyre, where Jesus meets the Syrophoenician women, was not the first of these incursions, as Mark tells it. Earlier, before this, Jesus crossed the Sea of Galilee (stilling a storm on the way) to go to "the country of the Gerasenes." This was part of the Decapolis: *gentile* country. That the demoniac was set free there with a "great herd of swine feeding" on the hillside, vividly underscored that this was very far from being a kosher zone! (4:35—5:20).

Furthermore, even while Jesus was still in Galilee—before he made his departures from spiritual home territory—he was already healing gentiles. Notice, very early on, the description of those who came to Jesus "in

"Grant Us, O Lord, to Trust in You with All Our Hearts"

great numbers." In addition to "a great multitude from Galilee . . . they came to him in great numbers from Judea [and] Jerusalem." So far, areas populated by our Lord's fellow Jews. But the text continues: "And from Idumea, and beyond the Jordan, and the vicinity of Tyre and Sidon" (3:7–8). These are all non-Jewish places, not home country. Jesus, at this introductory stage in the narrative, had not yet gone out to their own population centers. But he was already healing gentiles who came to him.

Throughout his Gospel, Mark pays close attention to geography, and he will make a point of noting when our Lord goes to boundaries—and when our Lord goes *across* boundaries.

It's really quite wonderful all that can be found in the text if we—especially those who preach, teach, or write—pay attention.

God's redemptive work was *always* meant to reach out to the whole world when "the time was fulfilled" (1:15), as was repeatedly emphasized in the Old Testament Scriptures. Through Israel, "all the families of the earth" would come to be blessed (Gen 12:3). This message was further emphasized in the prophets—in particular, Isaiah—which Jesus himself knew and loved with a special affection.

There are three additional factors to consider, to help us truly engage today's text—to help us take it to heart, as it was meant to be taken.

First, and regrettably this is disguised in a number of translations, in the entirely of Mark's Gospel—in its whole course, beginning to end—the Syrophoenician woman is the *only* person who directly addresses Jesus as "Lord" (7:28). That's something, isn't it? Perhaps even a decisive tip-off. It makes her much more appropriately seen as someone revealed to be an example of humble, trusting, and persistent faith—in Jesus, as he was.

Second, as is the case with any written text: we miss, of course, the tone of voice and facial expression. We feel this as a notable lack in a passage such as ours, where there's much more going on than what just meets our immediate reading eye. So, it's even more important to pay real attention to its larger picture, with all that it has to give us.

As a side note, this is why we can often get into trouble with things like texts and e-mail, isn't it? Our readers can't see our face or hear our voice. We can't see or hear them and respond to any evident confusion or distress on their part right way on the spot. Good reasons why, if we've keyed out a "whopper," it may be best to wait—maybe even sleep on it—before we click "send"!

And there is a *third* factor for us to consider, which will bring us back again to context. Here are the hard words of today's Scripture themselves once more:

> He said to her, "Let the children be fed first, for it is not fair to take the children's food and throw it to the dogs." But she answered him, "Lord, even the dogs under the table eat the children's crumbs." (7:27–28)

In a situation with a limited household food supply, it would be evident that we would—and should!—feed our children before we feed our puppy. That's completely evident.

Yet shortly before today's episode, Jesus fed the five thousand (6:30–44). And very shortly after, he feeds the four thousand (8:1–10). If you'll pardon the expression, we might say that the passage we're considering this morning is *sandwiched* between the two stories of miraculous feeding! This is part of Mark's point. And setting aside our own cultural biases, at least enough to give this text an honest, in-context, good-faith, and open hearing, should make things a good deal clearer for us.

There's still some mystery—and perhaps a measure of discomfort too. We're still not fully sure of all that Jesus was up to in his conversation with this mother in distress: not fully sure of why, exactly, he did things as he did. But the big picture does give us full reason "to trust in him with all our heart."

The gospel truth is that with him, and from him, and in him, there is—and there will be—an inexhaustible supply of bread. He *has* it to give, and he has the *capacity* and *willingness* to give. There is—and will be—plenty enough for everyone. "The time is fulfilled" (1:15). The question is: Will we "be opened," (7:34) to receive it? Or might we better ask, Will we be opened to receive him, who is himself the bread of life? (John 6:35ff).

Before today's story in the Gospel narrative, Jesus has *already* been healing gentiles, albeit at home; he has already gone out from home, crossing the boundary into foreign places, to heal there, too. And he has already just "fed the children," in miraculous abundance, with plenty left over. So then: What might all this have to tell us about his encounter with the Syrophoenician woman?

It tells us that it was no mere accident. It's full of the whole story's great purpose. And no, it's certainly *not* an account of an unclear or confused Jesus somehow having to be challenged, educated, or brought to more "evolved" status. And no, neither is it a story of our Lord's own discernment, in terms of the scope of his mission. His own actions so far, as Mark sets them down, have already started to make that quite clear, in letters writ large. But today's passage, even with its discomfort, certainly sends that message home—the message of the full scope of Jesus' mission; it sends it "home" (wherever and whatever that now might be for us), once again for us, in vividness and great power.

And Mark, as he continues from here, will underscore it more and more, as his Gospel's great refrain.

So, no matter how "far off" you find yourself, no matter how out-of-bounds you might feel or even how much of an outsider you may be to this whole church-project, Jesus came—and Jesus *comes*—with salvation and healing, with gracious summons to enter his realm of new life—just for the likes of you. That's what many of us who are already "here" have discovered, in joy, for ourselves. For Christ, the Son of God, there is no "too far" or "too hard."

Today's episode, with the gentile woman in such great need, is most likely an acted-out parable of Jesus, similar to some of those from the prophets of old, which both tests and teaches. By this, *the woman herself* was tested—perhaps even in some evident affection—and shown thereby to be an example of faith, both for insiders and outsiders.

Those of us who've been around for a while in the Episcopal Church may recall the classic Prayer of Humble Access, recited before the reception of holy communion. It's still used in Rite I.[3] Some may find this prayer an unhelpful relic of the past. I actually find it deeply encouraging. One of its phrases is a spin-off from her words:

> We are not worthy so much as to gather up the crumbs under thy Table.

The disciples of Jesus were tested, as well; challenged to understand the scope of what Christ was doing, more deeply and fully. Again, from the Prayer:

> But thou art the same Lord whose property is always to have mercy.

And, by extension, *we who hear this Gospel story today* are being tested too. We are being invited to "trust in our Lord with all our hearts" even—and especially—when things do not yet seem to make full sense.

---

3. *Book of Common Prayer*, 337.

> Grant us . . . gracious Lord, so to eat the flesh of thy dear Son Jesus Christ, and drink his blood, that we may evermore dwell in him, and he in us.

We often get the order of things spiritually wrong. In faith, it's not "learn to the full extent of our personal satisfaction" and after that, we'll start to parcel out our trust, bit by bit, usually on some probationary basis. Now, in our human relationships, maybe this is sometimes how it has to be. But with God, we can only really learn when we've already begun to trust. "Be opened!" Then receive the gift. That's how it works. In our faithful discipleship, this is key.

When we're "on top of the world"—or when we're still pretty determined to see ourselves as up there—gospel interpretations which put us in the position of knowing more than Jesus does may have their allures. We're feeling good about ourselves, and we know "what's what." Why risk interference? Perhaps we might be very tempted to go with an alternate, innocuous "Jesus" who isn't there. But there are many times too—many situations, in these vulnerable, hurting lives of ours—when, deep down, we may be given to understand that we need the Jesus who knows *more* than we do and who knows what he's doing—and for our good. We need *this* Jesus—who's very much there.

Furthermore, this is the One, not only with the knowledge we don't have, but also with the *will* and the *competence* to accomplish his good purpose for us. I'll stress those words: "his good purpose." To be sure, we may often not understand what he's doing—or why he's doing what he's doing and why he's not doing what he's not. That can be hard. There will be plenty of mystery that you and I will have to live with. More times than we would prefer, we'll be stretched, our prior "understandings" probed and challenged. It'll be an adventure, to be sure; a "Pilgrim's Progress," I should hope.

But by grace, I will trust this Lord. And I pray that you will, too.

"Rivers of Living Water"
Virtual Sermon, Columbia Falls, Montana

Pentecost, Year A: 1 Cor 12:3–13, John 7:37–39, and Ezek 47:1–12
Sunday, May 31, 2020

ALLELUIA! CHRIST IS RISEN!

We come, in the mercy of God, to "the last day of the festival," Pentecost, the culmination of the great fifty days of Easter. However, the circumstances of this year's Pentecost are disconcerting—to say the least—aren't they? Much of the church is unable to gather in person. And we come to this day in the midst of profound national distress. Great urgencies are demanding our attention; necessarily so.

What must we *do* in order to make a godly difference in this gravely wounded world?

That's an apt and very necessary question. Yet we must take some care, too, that the constant series of the "urgent" does not so consume us that we never get to other matters, often speaking with the "still, small voice" (1 Kgs 19:12 KJV) of the Spirit, which are, nevertheless, still colossally *important*—perhaps right in front of us yet all too often overlooked. After all, it is frequently the case that our desperate urgencies will find no healthy resolution until we reconnect with some important things that we've allowed ourselves to forget.

This, I'm convinced, is where the church is meant to come in. In the midst of all things, and empowered in the Spirit, "we must be about our Father's business" (Luke 2:49).

And so, calling upon mercy, let's get to it.

I should like to begin by drawing your attention—as my own attention has been drawn—to the opening words of one of the options for the second lesson of Pentecost: that is First Corinthians, chapter 12; verse 3.

From the East Gate

No one can say "Jesus is Lord" except by the Holy Spirit.

To be sure, the whole passage that follows is worthy of extended attention, but I suggest a focus on these opening words.

But I much regret having to make note of the increasingly popular distancing-away from the use of the word "Lord" in our devotion. As will become clear, I don't view this development as a healthy one. Not at all.

"Lord" is frequently being replaced, these days, with either "God" or "Savior," as though these three words—Lord, God, and Savior—were simply interchangeable synonyms. They are not. Each of them has its own distinctive range of meaning. Each of them has its own irreplaceable part to play in our historic vocabulary of faith.

To call him "Lord"—and of course, we aren't talking about a talisman, or a mere vocalization of some magic word—to call him "Lord" doesn't come naturally to any of us. That we should be able to call him "Lord" is God's gift: a sovereign, gracious, and mysterious gift, given to us through the regenerating power of God's Spirit.

To call him "Lord"—in the full depth of what this means—is *a first sign* of our lively incorporation into the "Pentecostal" baptism in the Spirit. It's not for nothing that the church's earliest creed—and still, I think, its most fundamental creed—is, precisely, "Jesus is Lord."

But what does it mean?

First, it's unique. If he is Lord, nothing else, and no one else is: not Caesar, not the "powers and principalities" (Eph 6:12 KJV)—whatever these might be—in us or around us, and not either the "best"—or the worst—of any of our own stuff.

Not even the church is "Lord." Such a thing would be an institutional monstrosity of the sort advocated by Dostoevsky's Grand Inquisitor.

So, the kingdom of Christ is direct: unbrokered and unmediated. Nothing can or ought to separate us from our share in its perfect care. It is to be our first and ultimate allegiance. Jesus Christ is to be the fountain, the definition, and the destination of our identity.

Let's delve, now, into some specifics of what this uniqueness means.

The English word, "Lord" translates the Hebrew word אדון ['adon] and the Greek word Κυριος [*kyrios*]. In Latin, it's Dominus. We need to note that all words, in their own languages, have their own histories—and their own distinctive ranges of meaning. So, when translating from one language to another, the best one can do is to go for close matches, rather than exact equivalents.

"Rivers of Living Water"

However, in the sweep of Jewish and Christian faith across the centuries, there has been substantial interplay between the terms אדון [*'adon*] and Κυριος [*kyrios*], their meanings thereby being further enriched and deepened: becoming charged, as we might say, with God's grandeur. "Dominus" and "Lord," in Latin and English (not to mention other tongues), have in their turn been caught up in that process.

We certainly don't have time for extended etymological study! However, I do want to underscore, in particular, that while in the process of biblical usage these words pick up the most profound cosmic significance, in their roots—and also as a key part of their ongoing meaning—they are *household* terms. In their own ways, they each denote someone who leads and cares for a household. They are terms of *immediate relationship*. An aspect of our word "Lord" that I especially cherish is its derivation from the word in Old English for "loaf-bearer"[1]—the one who provides the family its bread. Loaf-bearer: how aptly this coheres with Jesus, who gives the bread that he himself is, for "the life of the world" (John 6:51).

He is already the rightful Lord of all things. But to "call" Jesus "Lord," in faith, is to recognize him for who he is—*and who he is for us*. It means to be in living relationship with him: practically and directly, personally and in fellowship. It means that our allegiance—immediately and ultimately—is to him. It means that we cherish his leadership and trust, utterly, in his protection and provision. It means, in short, that we know ourselves to be a part of his great household.

But we can't "work all this up" in ourselves, on our own steam. Because,

> No one can say "Jesus is Lord" except by the Holy Spirit.

So, from one of our Pentecost hymns, my prayer for you—and for me—is,

> Like the murmur of the dove's song, like the challenge of her flight,
> like the vigor of the wind's rush, like the new flame's eager might:
> Come, Holy Spirit, come![2]

Let's turn now to the passage from the seventh chapter of John, today's Feast Day gospel reading. To refresh our memories, let's hear again:

> On the last day of the festival, the great day, while Jesus was standing there, he cried out, "Let anyone who is thirsty come to me,

---

1. Hlāfweard.
2. *Hymnal 1982*, #513.

and let the one who believes in me drink. As the scripture has said, 'Out of the believer's heart shall flow rivers of living water.'" Now he said this about the Spirit, which believers in him were to receive. (7:37–39)

"Out of the believer's heart shall flow rivers of living water." What a promise to those who come to him, those who believe in him. How wonderful! Jesus likely offered here a loose citation from the prophet Isaiah (58:11).

But I strongly suspect that he also had in mind a passage from another prophet as well: Ezekiel, chapter 47, verses 1 through 12. Technically, it isn't one of the lessons appointed for Pentecost. But I think that it should be! Very regrettably, it never comes up *anywhere* in our three-year Sunday lectionary. It's a part of Ezekiel's vision of the New Temple, from which living, healing, and restoring waters will flow.

When these enter . . .

> the sea of stagnant waters, the water will become fresh. Wherever the river goes, every living creature that swarms will live, and there will be very many fish, once these waters reach there. It will become fresh; and everything will live where the river goes . . . On the banks, on both sides of the river, there will grow all kinds of trees for food. Their leaves will not wither nor their fruit fail, but they will bear fresh fruit every month, because the water for them flows from the sanctuary. Their fruit will be for food, and their leaves for healing.

Is Jesus saying that all this—the New Temple from which the restoring waters flow—is what his faithful people would become? Yes, I think so.

To be sure, in John's Gospel it's fully clear that Jesus himself is the New and Perfect Temple. (2:21) And from his crucified side flowed the life-giving stream. (19:34)

Yet we are now in him, and he in us. We, too, are now his body. On Pentecost, the church was baptized in the same Spirit sent down upon him, at his Baptism in the River Jordan.

Saint Paul said, "Do you not know that [you are] a temple of the Holy Spirit within you?" (1 Cor 6:19).

To underscore this, even more, here are two additional New Testament passages.

From Ephesians, chapter 2, verses 19 through 22:

> You are no longer strangers and aliens, but you are citizens with the saints and also members of the household of God, built upon the foundation of the apostles and prophets, with Christ Jesus himself as the cornerstone. In him the whole structure is joined together and grows into a holy temple in the Lord; in whom you also are built together spiritually into a dwelling place for God.

And from First Peter, chapter 2, verses 4 and 5:

> Come to him, a living stone, though rejected by mortals yet chosen and precious in God's sight, and like living stones, let yourselves be built into a spiritual house, to be a holy priesthood, to offer spiritual sacrifices acceptable to God.

And once again, from today's Epistle,

> Now there are varieties of gifts, but the same Spirit; and there are varieties of services, but the same Lord; and there are varieties of activities, but it is the same God who activates all of them in everyone. To each is given the manifestation of the Spirit for the common good. (12:4–7)

In Christ, the perfect meeting place of God and humankind, *we too* become "temple." The world is in great need of that temple: the temple of those who live in the lordship of Jesus. So the church owes the world a good deal more than merely repeating back at it (perhaps with a bit of generic "spirituality" tossed in) the world's own "talking points."

The people who live in the lordship of Jesus are releasing a new way of being into the world. If Jesus is Lord (and nothing else is, and no one else is), his people must *never* indulge the notion that the persons and situations right in front of us—in our immediate here-and-now—"don't count." We need to be careful about this because there isn't *anyone* of us who isn't liable—very liable—to the notion that "the ends (simply) justify the means" because things are really hard, or that we're feeling so very strongly, or even, that our cause is comparatively righteous.

> No one can say "Jesus is Lord" except by the Holy Spirit.
> Come, Holy Spirit, come.

We are to be a people of un-extinguishable hope: right now, in the face of everything, and to all eternity.

> If you confess with your lips that Jesus is Lord and believe in your heart that God raised him from the dead, you will be saved. (Rom 10:9)

As great a personal promise as this is—and it is very great, indeed!—there's more to it than merely getting individual benefits and then going on our way. By God's amazing grace, we—the likes of *us*—are being formed into a temple from which the waters will flow.

All of creation will be restored to its place in the household of God, under the care of its rightful Lord. In God's eternal purpose, it's already a "done deal." But in his good pleasure, we get to be in on making it so.

Out of *your* hearts shall flow rivers of living water.

You may ask: But what, then, are we going to *do*? Well, many things, of course, all held in the One Great Thing.

Nevertheless, I bid us, as the people who call Jesus "Lord," to remember—always remember—whose business we must be about (see Luke 2:49 KJV). Occasionally, there will be some serious figuring out in store for us, as we discern the way in the midst of all the difficulties.

But a good deal of it is already as plain as day, isn't it?

The Lord is risen indeed! Alleluia!

"Wages or Free Gift"
A Virtual Sermon, Columbia Falls, Montana

Proper 8, Year A: Rom 6:12–23
Sunday, June 8, 2020

Today I should like to draw our attention to the closing sentence of this Sunday's second lesson: the letter of Paul to the Romans, chapter six, verse twenty-three.

> For the wages of sin is death, but the free gift of God is eternal life in Christ Jesus our Lord.

There's so much packed into these few words that we have to admit, right away, that we can't get anywhere near to exhausting their meaning. All that we can hope to do, and that by the power of the Spirit, is to indicate a way into engaging that meaning—and then trusting that same Spirit to lead us on, from there.

It may help, as we begin, to pull the camera back a bit. From early on in Romans, Paul has been very concerned to protect his readers from possible misunderstandings of the gospel; in particular, misunderstandings of God's grace, and how God's grace works. Paul has been taking on the distortion of The Message, which allows people to tell themselves, "Let us do evil so that good may come" (3:8). The gospel is not a private arrangement that we strike with God, that provides personal benefits (of sorts) but does not change—and does not govern—how we then are to live.

Paul is stressing that to receive the gospel is to experience a decisive transfer from one realm (or one way of being) to another—and that God, in Christ, is the one who has accomplished this. It is God's saving power, through Christ's cross, which has borne us into the new and eternal way of being. And yes, that is "all of grace":[1] free, unmerited gift.

Nevertheless, from that point on, we are summoned to live, to act, and to "be" in such a way as to manifest, more and more, the life-saving change that God has wrought in us. We now are to "present ourselves to God as those who have been brought [by him] from death to life" (6:13).

Paul knows full well that we will forget from time to time—that we will wander off into this detour or that and then stand much in need of correction and renewal. Paul knows that we are, at present, living (sometimes frustratingly) in between "the already and the not-yet." Yet Paul is also clear—and wants us to be clear—that at the heart of it, there is a radical distinction between the two realms of being. They are, fundamentally, utterly at odds with each other.

> For the wages of sin is death, but the free gift of God is eternal life in Christ Jesus our Lord.

Let's hear a portion of what Paul wrote in Romans, chapter six, *before* we get to today's verse:

> What then are we to say? Should we continue in sin in order that grace may abound? By no means! How can we who died to sin go on living in it? Do you not know that all of us who have been baptized into Christ Jesus were baptized into his death? Therefore we have been buried with him by baptism into death, so that, just as Christ was raised from the dead by the glory of the Father, so we too might walk in newness of life . . . Should we sin because we are not under law but under grace? By no means! Do you not know that if you present yourselves to anyone as obedient slaves, you are slaves of the one whom you obey, either of sin, which leads to death, or of obedience, which leads to righteousness? But thanks be to God that you, having once been slaves of sin, have become obedient from the heart to the form of teaching to which you were entrusted, and that you, having been set free from sin, have become slaves of righteousness. I am speaking in human terms because of your natural limitations. For just as you once presented your members as slaves to impurity and to greater and greater iniquity, so now present your members as slaves to righteousness for sanctification. (6:1–4, 15–19)

---

1. Allusion, here, to Charles Spurgeon's *All of Grace*.

"Wages or Free Gift"

We don't like to think of ourselves as being "in service." We're "free agents." We're the employers—not the employees—of the universe, aren't we? And if there are "wages" to be paid, we're the ones to be doing the paying—even to God himself—aren't we?

Yeah, sure.

Yes, for the time being, we're a mixed bag, but ultimately, and at heart, "no one can serve two masters" (Matt 6:24). So, what's it going to be—sin or grace?

It might be helpful at this point, to ponder what it is that we mean when we say the word "sin."

Let me address some common misunderstandings.

First, we tend to reduce "sin" to mere personal "rule-breaking," but in fact, the biblical view is that sin is *anything* that runs counter to what God wills for us. And since God is the One Who Is Our Life, when we detach from him, we are detaching ourselves from our own life—and, by definition, sentencing ourselves to death. In fact, "sin" (in all its manifestations, large and small) is an antagonistic cosmic power, determined to hold its captives in its sway.

We also tend to reduce our concept of "sin" so that it includes only individual transgression. But sin infects the entire human community, as community. Sin is, by definition, "systemic"—and universally so. It is both personal and communal. In it, we are—*all of us*—mired and enmeshed.

We also tend to reduce our concept of "sin" to include only that which is obviously unworthy—all that which is obviously selfish, indulgent, or unjust. To be sure, such things certainly are sinful. Yet sin can also commandeer what seems to be the most noble, the most necessary and most righteous of our endeavors. I can't stress this enough. And sin precisely in its seemingly "positive" manifestations can often be at its most pernicious and destructive. Satan is really good at masquerading as an "angel of light" (2 Cor 11:14).

Lastly, we tend to reduce our concept of "sin" so that—amazingly—it only applies to "others" whom we don't like: never (really) us—not "our kind" and not those whose approval we are craving.

And we must not think that those who have come to Christ get an immediate immunity to all this. It's a sadly effective tactic of sin to tell those in Christ, who are in the *process* of being freed from its power—a process that will continue as long as this present life continues—that it, sin, is still somehow necessary—or at the least, justifiable.

"You *need* me," sin says. "Let me be your tool, that God's 'will be done, on earth, as it is in heaven.' Let's make a deal. I'll be nice, this time around. 'Do evil, that good may prevail.'"

"God forbid!" (6:2 KJV).

God, give us the grace to see sin for what it is: a cosmic con artist. God, grant that we see that sin will happily lead human persons and human community from bad to lots, lots worse, indulging our sense of self-righteousness every step of the way. That's a con that sin especially likes.

But may we know, in the mercy of God, that the tactics of hell will *never* get us to heaven. For Christians, there can be no "strategic alliances" with sin. In spite of our now provisionally blended existence, at the heart of things we are facing an either-or. Remembering this is not meant to make us proud or judgmental but rather clear-headed. Or maybe I should say, "clear-hearted." In the words of a very early Christian writing: "There are two Ways [of being]: a Way of Life and a Way of Death, and the difference between these two Ways is great."[2] Those living in the lordship of Jesus should know where we're going—and how we get there.

So, I pray that you and I may know—and know, at gut level—that indulging sin fits the classic definition of insanity: of doing the same thing, repeatedly, and somehow expecting different results. Because "the wages of sin is death."

Sin does "pay a wage," as our text says. But notably, in the range of the Greek original, that word can have a connotation of *the rations of a slave*. Very apt, here, I think, when considering Paul's context. We like to think of ourselves as the *employers* of all things—God included. Truth is, though, that in our unregenerate life, we're not even employees but captives who get tossed a ration. And what are those rations? Death.

By definition, then, whether we recognize it at the time or not, sin pulls us away from Being.

"But [thanks,] thanks be to God" (1 Cor 15:57). We who had been on the "Going-Nowhere-Fast" Express have now been borne into the Pilgrim's Progress.

> For the wages of sin is death, but the free gift of God is eternal life in Christ Jesus our Lord.

In the midst of bitter debates about whose lives we now may say "matter"—in the midst of all this world's clashing strategies and tactics, I bid you

---

2. *Didache*, 1.1. Louth, *Early Christian Writings*, 191.

to *remember*. Today, tomorrow, forever: in all circumstances, "the free gift of God"—for you and for anyone you could ever possibly meet—"is eternal life in Christ Jesus our Lord."

A different way of being, a different kind of life: that's what God has in store for us. Not a false accommodation to "the way things were" before Christ, outside of Christ. Not a mere anesthetic, administered to the passengers on the "Going Nowhere Fast" Express. (That's the message of the phony gospel of "niceness.")

So, how do we get to "the life that really is life"? (1 Tim 6:19).

Here's the deal: *there is no "deal."* The only way we get to that life, first of all, is by God's free gift: grace. *God's* grace, received then passed along. His "free gift . . . is eternal life." Starting right now. Therefore,

> you also must also consider yourselves dead to sin and alive to God in Christ Jesus. (6:11)

Alive unto God: in the midst of all confusion, in the face of all contradiction, and in spite of every setback, this is to be our zeal, our uttermost desire. No substitutes!

When in risk of being "conned" once again—either from the right or from the left—then, by the power of God, we remember: we return to the "Faithful and True," the "Amen"; the One in whom "every one of God's promises is a Yes" (Rev 19:11; 3:14, 2 Cor 1:20).

The free gift, alive unto God, in "whose service" only "is perfect freedom."[3]

Why should we settle for anything else?

---

3. See "A Collect for Peace," Morning Prayer, *Book of Common Prayer*, 57, composed by Thomas Cranmer from the Sacramentary of Pope Gelasius I.

"Puddleglum's Testimony"
A Virtual Sermon, Columbia Falls, Montana

Proper 14, Year A: Rom 10:6–13
August 9, 2020

> Do not say in your heart, "Who will ascend into heaven?" (that is, to bring Christ down) or "Who will descend into the abyss?" (that is, to bring Christ up from the dead). [For] the word is near you. (Rom 10:6)

It is not for us, not for the likes of us, to haul salvation down—as an acquired treasure that we "get." Neither is it for us to haul our salvation up—as some sort of rescue operation that we manage to pull off. And "Christ" is not a pious word for what *we* aspire to achieve, spiritually or socially. But the sad truth is that our inclination is to replace "the righteousness that comes from faith" with our own so very well-intentioned projects.

Deep down, but perhaps seldom admitted, we fear that we won't be good enough to succeed, and so we reel back and forth between the closely related polarities of zealotry and shame.

But in the midst of the unhappy dance of these polarities, God breaks in: *God* purchases, once again, what was already his. He rescues what had rebelliously departed from his perfect care. The Word came near. Have we heard—gratefully, lovingly, utterly heard—so that it be in our hearts and on our lips?

If so, then we are no longer the captive property of our various fanaticisms—and we no longer need be tortured or manipulated by shame. For "everyone who calls on the name of the Lord shall be saved" (Rom 10:13, quoting Joel 2:32).

"Puddleglum's Testimony"

There is a terrible, in fact humanly inescapable, solidarity in sin. But also, in the gospel promise, a radical equality: "The same Lord is Lord of all and is generous to all who call on him." But "what part of *all* do we not yet understand?" And "what part of all do we not *wish* to understand? Who is it—maybe, so very sadly, sometimes even our own selves—whom we are tempted to leave to the devises of this shame-mongering world?

One of my favorite passages in all of C. S. Lewis' writings is the climactic scene from *The Silver Chair*. The children, Jill and Eustace, along with Puddleglum, the Marshwiggle, are seeking the lost Prince, Rilian. They've found him, deep underground, in their adversary's dungeon. But they're captives at this point in the story, and they're being subjected to a highly convincing serenade in which they're being told that Narnia—the world on the earth above, from which they've actually come—just doesn't exist! Neither is there such a thing as Aslan, that world's rightful creator and lord. Such ideas are just a distraction from the only real business at hand. Frighteningly, the prisoners are just about convinced: the prison is all there is.

"There never was any world but mine," said the Witch. Essentially, she's saying, "You may doubt all else, but never me." All other "orthodoxies" may be questioned and resisted—and I'll happily encourage you to do so—but never mine. Go ahead, deride anything that you want to label as "fundamentalist" (or whatever pejorative fits your preference), just as long as you give *my* fundamentalism your total, unqualified allegiance.

By the way, does that just happen to sound a bit like what's increasingly being demanded of people in the contemporary sociopolitical arenas?

To return to the story, the episode comes to a decisive turning point, the disenchanting spell is broken, and Puddleglum—a character much after my own heart—says these remarkable words to the Witch:

> "Suppose we *have* only dreamed, or made up, all those things—trees and grass and sun and moon and stars and Aslan himself. Suppose we have. Then all I can say is that, in that case, the made-up things seem a good deal more important than the real ones. Suppose this black pit of a kingdom of yours is the only world. Well, it strikes me as a pretty poor one. And that's a funny thing, when you come to think of it. We're just babies making up a game, if you're right. But four babies playing a game can make a play-world which licks your real world hollow."[1]

Wonderful!

---

1. Lewis, *Silver Chair*, 182.

We Christians no longer have to be captives to fear. No longer do we have to give mindless consent to this world's competing "catechisms," which, in spite of their bitter mutual antagonisms, are far more like each other than they'd ever want to admit—just ringing changes on the same old, tired, fleshly, human-powered agendas of fixing and acquisition, just the will to power in an arbitrary, zero-sum universe.

In Jesus Christ, we are tapped into something radically different: an abundance—a hope—that "licks the phony 'real' world hollow." So, Christians no longer need be captives to shame either: not shame's tortures, nor its tactics of manipulation, imposed on us by ourselves or others.

Repentance, yes, absolutely: as profound—as utter—as radical—as it must be! Repentance is God's gift: it's the handmaid of salvation filled, by definition, with the hope of new beginning and the promise of freedom. It leads us back to belonging.

Shame, on the other hand, just leads to more captivity. It's something that we impose on ourselves, socially or personally. And—even when huddled with others, desperate to create their own utopias, but who also are quietly terrified that they'll never really measure up—the way of shame means that at the end of the earthly day, everybody is still alone.

But the Word has come near us, and through him, in him, by him, God has acted. Repent and believe. So, "do not say in your heart, 'Who will ascend into heaven? (that is, to bring Christ down) or 'Who will descend into the abyss?' (that is, to bring Christ up from the dead)." You do not need, by your own well-intentioned—but still desperate—efforts of acquisition or of fixing, to haul Christ down, or haul him up. Because he—the Word—has already come near. He is near. And he is near *you*. Directly near you. Unbrokered, unmediated—because he himself is the one Mediator.

No one needs to work through any special privileged class—or any class of "counter-privilege," for that matter—to get to him. The materialistic world knows only one way of getting things right. And that always involves earthly brokers. If there are problems, just make the "nice" people the brokers. It doesn't work, of course. It can't. Because *no one* is that thoroughly "nice." That's why all materialistic, zero-sum determinations to make an earthly paradise have ended up somewhere on the scale between injury and atrocity.

> All have sinned and fall short of the glory of God. (3:23)

Yet by God's generous mercy in Christ, "where sin increased, grace [has] abounded all the more" (5:20).

> "There is no distinction . . . the same Lord is Lord of all and is generous to all who call on him. For, 'Everyone who calls on the name of the Lord shall be saved.'"

The company of those who—at long last—have experienced gracious generosity, discover, amazingly, that they are also able to be generous in turn. They have discovered that reality isn't zero-sum, after all. These are they who are able to live like Narnians—able to live like the citizens of God's kingdom that they are. These are they who keep near, in greatest joy, to the One who has come near to them.

I want to be in that number. How about you?

"Strive to Be Found by Him at Peace"

All Saints Church, Columbia Falls, Montana

The Second Sunday of Advent, Year B: 2 Pet 3:8–15a
December 6, 2020

I INVITE OUR ATTENTION, this morning, to today's appointed New Testament lesson: the passage from the Second Letter of Peter. As we heard, it deals with the second coming of Christ. Of all Christian doctrines, that of Christ's second coming is one with which we stand in uneasy relationship. Many of us—maybe even most of us—aren't quite sure what to do with it. And frankly, what some folks *have* done with it has been unhelpful. That's putting it politely.

Nevertheless, this doctrine certainly seems to be hard-wired into the core of our faith: "He will come again in glory to judge the living and the dead, and his kingdom will have no end,"[1] as we recite almost every Sunday. But that's the *Nicene* Creed, isn't it? Well, here in the *Apostles'* Creed, "He will come again to judge the living and the dead."[2] And both of these simply draw from material from throughout the New Testament. Immediately following the account of the ascension in the book of Acts, the angels tell the apostles, "Men of Galilee . . . This Jesus, who has been taken up from you into heaven, will come in the same way as you saw him go into heaven" (1:11). And there are many more New Testament passages, much more than we have time to cite now, often extended passages, frequently from the lips of our Lord himself that speak of it as well.

---

1. *Book of Common Prayer*, 358.
2. *Book of Common Prayer*, 96.

And our present season in the church year, Advent, which we Episcopalians cherish so much, is largely devoted to this very same theme. That's why this particular lesson from Second Peter is given to us to hear today.

But even at its most responsible articulation, the doctrine of Christ's second coming leaves many of us feeling nonplussed, doesn't it? There's an illustration I sometimes used to use in regard to this, perhaps more apt for the days before COVID, when we could have large family gatherings without thinking twice about it. But I'll offer it here, once again, anyway: the doctrine of the end-times, and of Christ's return, may sometimes feel to us like the crazy relative that we *have* to invite to Thanksgiving but that we still dearly wish would keep quiet at the dinner table.

So, there we are. But instead of pulling back from the doctrine, I'm going to bid us to lean in—yes, *lean in*—and see what good gift God may have in store for us.

Instead of trying to figure out what *we're* going to do with *it*, let's wait to see what *it* might do with *us*.

> Do not ignore this one fact, beloved, that with the Lord one day is like a thousand years, and a thousand years are like one day. The Lord is not slow about his promise, as some think of slowness, but is patient with you, not wanting any to perish, but all to come to repentance. But the day of the Lord will come like a thief, and then the heavens will pass away with a loud noise, and the elements will be dissolved with fire, and the earth and everything that is done on it will be disclosed. (3:8–10)

A pastoral concern behind the writing of Second Peter, written already some time since our Lord's earthly ministry, was to address a particular set of questions arising among these still-early Christians: Why is Christ's promised return delayed? It's already been a while, now. Why is he not "getting to it," coming back, and setting things to right, right now? Why is he not yet dealing with this mess?

Throughout the long journey of God's people, we've all had to struggle with what certainly feels to us either like God's delay or his "inefficiency."

Well, what about it?

My first observation is that *their* questions then maybe aren't at all that radically different from *our* questions now. My second observation is that these questions, then and now, are only partially and indirectly answered by this morning's text. All this sort of stuff is dealt with in Scripture on a "need-to-know" basis. Not "really *want* to know" but "*need* to know."

There's a difference!

Why does God allow history—including our own personal stories—to play out as it does? The text doesn't go into any detail about this "why" but assures us that what seems like God's delay, God's inefficiency, has to do with a greater purpose—a greater mercy which we can't understand, at least not now.

> The Lord is not slow . . . as some think of slowness, but is patient . . . not wanting any to perish, but all to come to repentance.

I suggest that we consider, *first*, that for each of us, and for the world itself, an Ending is coming, and *second*, that we're not just personally and corporately waiting for it "all to be over," but we're waiting for *him*—waiting for him who promised to return in glory at a last judgment to heal, to restore, and to usher his redeemed creation into a living eternity. In all this, we're right at the frontier of what even inspired language can express—and (to say the least) we ought to be very cautious about trying to tack down systems and timetables. But we *are* speaking of a core dimension of our faith: a hope which is a part of the birthright of God's people, which we are meant to cherish (even if we barely can understand it).

Remember, it's not "want to know" but "need to know." And, truth to be told, we need much less detail about such things than we sometimes think we do.

Saint Augustine, at the end of his mammoth work, *The City of God*, puts this "need to know" in moving simplicity. He speaks of

> an eighth day, as it were, which is to last for ever, a day consecrated by the Resurrection of Christ . . . There we shall be still and see; we shall see and we shall love; we shall love and we shall praise. Behold what will be, in the end, without end! For what is our end but to reach that kingdom which has no end.[3]

> We wait for new heavens and a new earth, where righteousness is at home. (3:13)

So, maybe that crazy relative sitting at the corner of our Thanksgiving table, who we were hoping would just keep quiet, is actually a wise elder with something to say that we really need to hear.

Meanwhile:

---

3. Augustine, *City of God* 22.30 (Bettenson, 1091).

Before that blessed "then," an End *will* come, as it must. We—you and I—are mortal. We have life spans that begin and end. However, it's not just individual persons that die. So also do societies and civilizations. So also will this entire world. So also will our sun, solar system—and beyond. They all, in their own ways, have life spans that begin and end. This present life, at all levels, from small to vast, is a limited-run engagement. This present life, at all levels, from small to vast, is far more transient—and fragile—than we prefer to remember.

Endings are difficult. I'm not speaking here of mere "transitions" (even significant transitions) within some ongoing life system. Rather, I'm speaking of Endings with a capital *E*: in other words, *Deaths*. These are *difficult*, by definition. Sometimes much more so, sometimes—thankfully—somewhat less so. But there's something always traumatic—one might even say, *apocalyptic*—about capital *E* Endings. But God is both Alpha *and* Omega. It's not as though God brought all things into being and then somehow lost control. That would be "Alpha but *not* Omega." No, thanks be, our God is Alpha *and* Omega (Rev 1:8, 21:6, 22:3; see also Isa 44:6).

The God from whom we have our beginning is also the One who is taking in hand our End. "The Day of the Lord will come" for each and—ultimately—for the whole world.

But even in the midst of apocalyptic trauma, that day—in both its personal forms throughout time, and its global form at the end of time—comes "like a thief"—in other words: stealthily, unpredictably, unexpectedly.

We, however, as the Lord's people, are to live so as to "expect the unexpected." After all, we already know him! "Even so, come, Lord Jesus" (Rev 22:20 KJV).

We're not just waiting for it "all to be over." We're waiting for *him*. To be sure, even now, by the power of the Spirit, he is always with us. Yet it is also the case that

> now we see in a mirror, dimly, but then we will see face to face. Now I know only in part; then I will know fully, even as I have been fully known. (1 Cor 13:12)
>
> Beloved, we are God's children now; what we will be has not yet been revealed. What we do know is this: we will be like him, for we will see him as he is. (1 John 3:2)

Even so, come, Lord Jesus.

For each one of us personally, for everyone we know, for everyone we could possibly know, and indeed—finally—for all things, the question that begins one of John Donne's poems is always apt:

What if this present were the world's last night?[4]

And I think that our text gives us an essential part of the right answer to such a question:

Strive to be found by him at peace. (3:14)

But this present world seems *determined* to imprison us in constant states of agitation. In fact, it tells us that such states are the only way to get anything done. However, the all-too-sad truth is that the agitated, anxious, anger-addicted, irritated, passion-fueled, habitually resentful life—driven by various competing "derangement syndromes" (far more alike one another than we care to admit)—is a *diminishing* life: a "life" less and less alive and—inevitably—more and more destructive. Even with the very "best" of intentions. Even when we're so very sure that we are right.

Doesn't sound like what Jesus has in mind for us, does it?

We may wonder, though, if *striving* to be at *peace* is a bit of a contradiction. We can't exactly "white knuckle" our way to tranquility! True peace isn't something that we can hammer into being, either inside us or around us. Peace isn't really our "achievement," at all. Peace is a Person. "For he—Christ—is our Peace" (Eph 2:14).

So, I don't think that our text is a contradiction. Christ is, himself, both the gift of peace and the giver of peace. Our striving is grace-empowered reliance *on* him and ongoing return *to* him. So yes, indeed:

Strive to be found by him at peace.

By so doing, we become—not passive—but truly effective. In spite of the old saying to the contrary, maybe it is *only* by being heavenly minded that we, the church, can be of any earthly good. Living in Christly peace doesn't make us uncaring or uninvolved. By no means!

The world *needs* a people in it who know how to live in between the once and future coming of Jesus Christ. We *ourselves* are meant to be the "thin place" between all that which is ending, and the promised yet-to-be: a people already rejoicing in the foretaste of the eighth and eternal day who reflect some of its wonderful light, right into this day-diminishing world.

---

4. "Divine Meditations 13," in Donne, *Complete English Poems*, 314.

"Strive to Be Found by Him at Peace"

What sort of persons ought you to be in leading lives of holiness and godliness, waiting for and eagerly desiring the coming of the day of God? . . . Beloved, while you are waiting . . . strive to be found by him at peace, without spot or blemish; and regard the patience of our Lord . . . as salvation (3:11, 14, 15).

"Dear One, I Say to You, Arise"
All Saints Church, Columbia Falls, Montana

Proper 8, Year B: Mark 5:21–43
Sunday, June 27, 2021

THIS MORNING WE ARE given to hear the interlaced story of two miracles. Amazing, to be sure: the healing of a woman long burdened with an uncurable ailment—that rendered her ritually impure—and the raising of a little girl from death. When Jesus said, "The child is not dead, but sleeping," he was not referring to her condition in itself but her condition *in relation to* what he is shortly going to do—rather like what he says in the story of Lazarus in John's Gospel. (11:1–44)

In the passage we just heard, Jesus overcomes hopeless suffering, alienation, and death: inexpressibly wonderful for the two who were healed—and to all who loved them. But what does it mean to us *now*? Is this just an account of something that happened *back then*, that can only impress us at a distance but not really touch us in our own, very non-miraculous present? Why, after all, did we devote the time to listen to it—and why am I, and many in my position, talking about it?

Such questions are all the more keen when we remember that in our assembly here today (and all possible assemblies, anywhere), there are many among us who are bearing burdens for which there will be no earthly reprieve: the disease which won't get cured, an alienation that will remain unbridgeable, a beloved child who isn't coming back. Many are bearing such. Perhaps, in one way or another, most of us. And eventually, all.

So, what are we going to do with these miracle stories?

Where is *our* good news, this morning?

As we begin to grapple with this, it may be helpful to consider, briefly, what the miracles of Jesus are—*and what they aren't*. They are demonstrations of his sovereign, gracious Lordship over all. They are demonstrations of his utter power to vanquish the powers hostile to God and hostile to God's own. But they are *not* the sum total of all that God, in Christ, is doing—or is going to do. Far from it. Rather, the miracles of Jesus, like those we hear today, are signs of *all* that which he will surely accomplish, although so much of it yet remains unseen to us. After all, for the two healed today, this was an earthly reprieve, not (yet) eternal deliverance. Both of them, like everyone else healed or raised by Jesus, were still prone to this world's sufferings and still fully liable to death. So, we might say that Jesus' miracles—as wondrous as they were—are a fairly modest down payment for all that is yet to come. They are his given pledges to us, so that we may be sure that he is good for the balance! Christ is not doing *less* than we had hoped but vastly more.

The more apt question, therefore, was perhaps not what *we* were going to do with the miracles in the Gospel narratives but what *they* were going to do with *us*.

In fact, the Gospel stories of Jesus' miracles, like the two we hear in today's passage, have much to say to *us* who live in such a militantly demythologized world; a world determined to be no longer "charged with the grandeur of God?"[1]

Of all the four Gospels—Matthew, Mark, Luke, and John—Mark's, from which we hear today, is the most action-packed. All the Gospels give us teaching from our Lord (what he *says*), but percentage-wise, Mark devotes the greatest share of his attention to what Jesus *does*. Mark gives us a relentlessly forward-moving narrative: a series of purposeful, astounding events, leading to the cross and empty tomb; all parts of the one great event that Jesus Christ, the Son of God, is.

As in today's passage, there is much of the miraculous in this gospel. But you and I live in the midst of so much default-skepticism, don't we? It seems to have become important to modern-folk to think that we live in a closed-system world: that our "reality" is not liable to interruption from outside of itself. Moderns less-and-less like the idea of such an interruption, ever. Not even "then," in the time of the New Testament, and certainly not now. What business does even God have to interfere with things—let alone invade?

But the good news is that God, in Christ, *did* invade; that he *has* interfered. Our "reality," yours and mine, *has been* interrupted. The Time of

---

1. "God's Grandeur," in Hopkins, *Poems and Prose*, 27.

Jesus Christ, to which the Scriptures testify, broke through. His time now contains—and transfigures—all times.

By the way, in contrast to all other miracles, Christ's resurrection is of a vastly higher order. *He*, the victor over death, will *never* die again. The resurrection isn't a mere sign but the present accomplishment and breakthrough, in him, of an ultimate new reality, for which both the girl and the woman, even after their healings, would still have to wait. And we here this morning—that's true for us, as well. On those occasions when we're given an earthly reprieve, and also in all the many times when we don't, we're still waiting too—but with a difference. Because we have "seen the Coming of the Glory of the Lord"[2] and we have heard "the good news of Jesus Christ, the Son of God." Even in the midst of a still-burdened life, in Christ, things can never be the same.

Yes, we're living an "in-between" existence—aren't we?—in the "Shadowlands." In such lands, the sufferings are real. As W. H. Auden put it,

> "To those who have seen . . . however dimly . . . The Time Being is . . . the most trying time of all."[3]

Nevertheless, "By him, and with him, and in him,"[4] even our shadowlands are now dappled[5] by his life, his beauty: "the light shining in the darkness, which the darkness cannot overcome" (John 1:5).

Praise him.

What does all this mean for us? Many things. In fact, everything. But for now, I'll invite us to focus on these two: first, that we are enjoined to faith, and second, that we are called to witness.

In *all* things, even now, Jesus is speaking, and in the age to come, fully, Jesus *will* speak his word of salvation:

> "He took her by the hand and said . . . 'Little girl, I say to you, get up!'" (5:41)

How simple and utterly sovereign; how decisive, how tender—in the face of all things, no matter what: "Little girl—dear one—I say to you, arise." Starting right here, right now, but with more in store, beyond the present frame, than we can possibly imagine. For "the time being," we see

---

2. Julia Ward Howe, "Battle Hymn of the Republic."
3. Auden, *For the Time Being*, 64 ("The Flight into Egypt," III).
4. The Great Thanksgiving, Doxology, in *Book of Common Prayer*, 363, 369.
5. Allusion to Hopkins's poem "Pied Beauty," in Hopkins, *Poems and Prose*, 30–31.

"Dear One, I Say to You, Arise"

only a fraction of what his word will mean. Nevertheless, he is good for all of it—and will leave nothing undone.

Therefore believe.

> "Daughter, your faith has made you well." (5:43)
> "Do not fear, only believe." (5:36)

And *faith* is, for us, an ongoing, growing, sometimes-struggling, but progressively more cherishing, personal trust in Jesus: the One who *is* himself our salvation—the One who *has* spoken, and *will* speak, his loving and utterly effective Word.

This world's powers and principalities hurl their message at us constantly. Loss, injury, injustice, disappointment, and death say, "This is it; there'll be nothing else, and in our power you will remain." But "*He* speaks; and, listening to his voice, new life the dead receive, the mournful broken hearts rejoice, the humble poor believe."[6]

> "Dear one, I say to you, arise."

And those who have been enjoined to faith, and are living in the new reality to which faith connects us, are called to *witness*. Yes, witness.

Let's be up front, though, and admit that witnessing is something that makes many of us rather nervous. Let's further admit that at least some of the time, there may be good reasons for feeling this way. Maybe we've seen the sad effects of self-righteous spiritual bludgeoning, the unfortunate aftermath of an oh-so-sure-of-itself steam-rolling proselytism. It's all too easy to forget that with spiritual sharing, we are treading on most holy ground.

But maybe, as well, sometimes we can be just too polite—for our own good, or anyone else's. I score pretty high myself on the introversion scale. So, I like to think that those like me do have some good things to offer in the great human mix. But I also think that our particular church tradition might sometimes be too liable to taking spiritual introversion to a place of unhelpful imbalance.

If the very *last* thing a Christian would ever be found doing (outside of a worship service) is talking about Jesus—explicitly and specifically—maybe there's some real need to grow back into some balance. That old question comes to mind: if we were on trial for actually being a follower of Jesus Christ (as opposed to simply being a generically nice person), how much evidence would there be to convict us?

---

6. Charles Wesley, "O for a Thousand Tongues," in *Hymnal 1982*, #493.

Therefore, "Name him, Christians, name him!"[7] Yes, with humility, with respect, with gentleness, with care, and with sensitivity to the apt times and circumstances—but still, indeed, "Name him!"

But how about that bit from the end of our passage, where Jesus "strictly ordered" the girl's parents (and Peter, James, and John) to keep quiet about what had happened? That's a good question. No, it doesn't let us off from the call to witness, but it's a good question. In Mark's Gospel, this is one of a series of examples in which the identity of Jesus was still to be kept partly secret. Why so? Because the full meaning of who he was, and the full intention of what he was doing, could not be rightly understood outside the sweep of the entire Gospel story—leading to the cross and empty tomb.

Nevertheless, at where we are in today's part of the story, there was plenty of witnessing going on—inevitably so. Our text says of the woman who had been suffering for twelve long years:

> She had heard about Jesus. (5:27)

The fact that some unnamed others had been speaking about Jesus, about what he was doing and where he might be found, is part of her miracle's providential chain. And those who had been doing that speaking—which she heard and took to heart—perhaps never knew the amazing effect of their words.

Our Lord has called us to be his witnesses. But *how* he uses our witness he only discloses to us on a "need-to-know" basis. So, indeed, "Name him, Christians, name him!"

A world in which he may be named, in which even now—by the power of the Spirit—we may touch the hem of his garment, and in which he takes us by the hand, is no longer for us a closed system trapped in its own misery.

And even while we're still waiting for all it will mean for us, "by him, and with him, and in him," we find that these present Shadowlands can be pretty miraculous, after all.

"Dear ones, I say to you, arise."

---

7. Caroline Maria Noel, "At the Name of Jesus," in *Hymnal 1982*, #435.

"Listen, Then See"
All Saints Church, Columbia Falls, Montana

Proper 22, Year B: Heb 1:1–4; 2:5–12
Sunday, October 3, 2021

STARTING TODAY, WE'LL BE hearing portions from the Letter to the Hebrews as the New Testament lesson for the better part of the next two months—almost all the way to the end of this liturgical year. This Sunday, we begin right at the beginning:

> Long ago God spoke to our ancestors in many and various ways
> . . . but in these last days he has spoken to us by a Son. (1:1, 2)

So, Jesus Christ is what God has to say to us: his foundational and fulfilling Word. There is nothing to add, nothing left unsaid—and certainly nothing to correct. And he is utterly unique: the "appointed heir of all things, through whom the worlds were created. He is the reflection of God's glory and the exact imprint of God's very being, and he sustains all things by his powerful word."

So, using a key phrase used later in the Letter to the Hebrews, this speaking is "once for all" (10:10).

But we are not to confine this "once for all" to only a past utterance. True, God spoke to us by a Son, at a particular time and place, in a particular set of circumstances—and then communicated to us in his own appointed means. All these—the time, place, circumstances, and means—are certainly earthly: fully human. Yet even as such, they are the instruments of God's self-disclosure for all time.

The specific time of Jesus in his earthly ministry holds *all* times and places. We are always present to it, and it is always present to us. Because this once-for-all speaking is himself the living Word: "living and active" (4:12), not just in some confined "then," but always *now*.

"Jesus Christ is the same yesterday and today and forever" (13:8). The living Word is utterly constant: faithful and reliable. But we are also, always, to "ponder anew."[1] Sometimes that will mean challenge for us. But also surprise, wonder—and joy.

Jesus Christ is what God has to say to us.

We, then, are to be good listeners.

Martin Luther, writing in his *Commentary on Galatians*, asserted, "We are made Christians . . . by *hearing*."[2] I believe that he was right.

In faith, *hearing* is our primary sense. Our life now starts with listening to the God who has spoken to us in Jesus Christ.

I'll need to admit, though, that this assertion, that hearing is our primary sense in faith, comes to me with a measure of personal poignancy.

I am hearing-impaired and have been since birth. And the advance of years hasn't exactly improved matters. I'm colossally grateful that hearing aids do get me in the range of normal everyday hearing function. (Sometimes I call them "my bionic ears.") Nevertheless, it still isn't quite the same. I've always had to pay more attention to hear well. Ambient sounds are a particular challenge. Noisy settings are hard.

My impairment comes with a particular cost, as I deeply love music. But thanks be: I'm still fine with music that I'm really listening to. However, background music, blared in stores, for example, can drive me up the wall. Then again, what sometimes gets blared from the speakers is only marginally classifiable as "music," as far as I am concerned. More like well-marketed industrial product: "singing" of a sort, which somehow has less and less *song* in it.

But back to the point; if we may use the analogy: when it comes to listening to God, *all of us*, by definition, are spiritually "hearing-impaired." Profoundly so. Furthermore, even after the healing, restoring intervention of the Spirit, throughout this present life we will have to be deliberate—and pay more attention—in order to hear God well. Being his good listeners doesn't just come to us by the path of least resistance. All of this life's many "background noises" will be a risk, too; a challenge to our focus.

Faith is not a ticket to passivity. Our pilgrimage will certainly call forth all that has been given to us. But the Giver is the One who not only speaks

---

1. Joachim Neander, "Praise to the Lord, the Almighty," in *Hymnal 1982*, #390.
2. Luther, *Galatians*, 118 (3:2), emphasis mine.

"Listen, Then See"

but also creates the ears with which we may hear his "living and active Word." And he not only creates the ears with which we may hear but also wills to be *heard*.

So, in godly love, determination, and curiosity—may we *listen*. Then, having so listened, we are in a position to engage our spiritual sight, "looking to Jesus the pioneer and perfecter of our faith" (12:2).

He is the eternal Son and Word who became our brother and made us *his* brothers and sisters.

> He had to become like [us] in every respect, so that he might be a merciful and faithful high priest . . . tested as we are, yet without sin. (2:17; 4:15)

Therefore, look to him. In all places, at all times. In godly love and determination—look "to Jesus, the pioneer and perfecter of our faith." Look to him—first, front, and center—and then we will, at long last, see everything else aright. Including our own selves. Otherwise, we're just wandering around in a hall of mirrors.

I'd invite us now to ponder this curious phrase in our text: "but we do see Jesus" (2:9). Notice the present tense. Not only "saw" or "will see." "We *do* see." This is an assurance after the candid recognition of all that we do *not* presently see while we're on the way—all the "not yet" of God's good purpose for us. And at present, we see plenty of things distinctly *counter* to all our hopes for the "not yet." By our fleshly eyes, we certainly *don't* see him. By every *fleshly* perception, Jesus is now gone.

And our text this morning itself speaks of the mystery of Christ's ascension:

> When he had made purification for sins, he sat down at the right hand of the majesty on high. (1:3)

Nevertheless, we are assured, "we do see Jesus."

So, we must be talking about a different kind of perception—a Spirit-given, Spirit-enabled new kind of seeing. How do we get to this? It's a gift. Not an achievement, not some strained image we try to force into our tired eyes.

Yet here is the astounding assurance: in Spirit-graced, faith-channeled new sight, we may now see him, the eternal Son—who became our brother, who offered himself on the cross once for all, for the sins of the whole world. What our fleshly eyes can't perceive, the eyes of faith can: him, our brother who was crucified, now in his victorious life, enthroned in the heavenlies.

"The head that once was crowned with thorns is crowned with glory now."[3] Catch just a glimpse of this, and nothing else can ever look the same.

The theme of Christ's ascension is too-often sidelined in our piety. It isn't just the story of Jesus going away. He is taking *our own human nature* right to the throne of God. He is our "pioneer" who is "able for all time to save those who approach God through him, *since he always lives to make intercession for them*" (7:25).

The ascension takes us beyond the frontier of what human language can possibly express. But we still are to take great joy in it, and *see all things differently* in its light. This is why I find the snarky dismissals of our Lord's ascension in the literature of the popularizing skeptics so terribly unfortunate.

I'll risk using an illustration that draws from J. K. Rowling's *Harry Potter* series. The stories all revolve around young magic folk at their school for magic, Hogwarts Academy—centrally, of course, one of these students: Harry himself. Non-magic folk are termed "Muggles."

Well, if there really *were* two types of human beings, magic folk and Muggles, of course, God would fully love them both—and for them both, would have plenty of room in all his good purposes.

Nevertheless, I still would have a great deal of difficulty understanding how a Muggle—who not only was non-magic but also thought that there was *no such thing* as magic—would be, or would want to be, a Hogwarts professor. Just wouldn't make any sense: no more sense than someone trying to be a music teacher, having never heard a note.

But the way of "godly re-enchantment" is a pointed challenge to our usual way of "perception," with all its *willful*—sometimes *militantly* willful—impairments. Rather, we are speaking of *new* capacities, initiated and enabled by God's grace: a hearing and a seeing, once again, *as we were meant to hear and see.*[4]

Living into this doesn't just happen by following our path of least resistance. We're utterly dependent on God's grace, from start to finish, but we're not passive, either. Living into this new way will summon us to deliberate, ongoing commitment. We must take care to remain rightly centered on Christ, "laying aside" (12:1) every distraction and returning always to what has been so richly bestowed. Only in these will we find our present here-and-now re-infused with the glory of God.

---

3. Thomas Kelly, *Hymnal 1982*, #483.
4. Allusion, here, to Tolkien, *Tree and Leaf*, 36–70, esp. 58 ("On Fairy Stories").

"Listen, Then See"

"Hast thou not seen?"[5]

From the book of the prophet Isaiah:

> "Have you not known? Have you not *heard*? Has it not been told you? . . . Have you not understood? . . . You shall have a song, as in the night when a holy festival is kept; and gladness of heart." (40:21; 30:29)

Do we now perceive—even in Spirit—*everything* of the promised yet-to-come? Of course not.

Nevertheless, by such wondrous gift, we know whom we have seen—and *do* see—in faith: the One crucified for our redemption, now ascended in glory, bringing our case—now become *his*—to the very throne of heaven.

> "Long ago God spoke to our ancestors in many and various ways . . . but in these last days he has spoken to us by a Son."

> "Faith comes from what is heard." (Rom 10:17)

Therefore, listen. Persistently. Attentively. With the ears that God would give.

Then, see. See as we were meant to see, not just the projections of all our own stuff.

Leave the hall of mirrors; behold the wonder that God has in store! Look to Jesus—and in him, see everything else. As "children of God through faith" (Gal 3:26), "you shall have a song."

---

5. Joachim Neander, "Praise to the Lord," in *Hymnal 1982*, #390.

"Approach the Throne"
Christ Church, Kalispell, Montana

Proper 23, Year B: Heb 4:12–16 and Mark 10:23b-27
Sunday, October 10, 2021

I INVITE OUR ATTENTION to today's passage from the Letter to the Hebrews. Even though it was just excellently read, it's so rich—so packed with meaning—that before we launch in, it's worth hearing again for a second time:

> The word of God is living and active, sharper than any two-edged sword, piercing until it divides soul from spirit, joints from marrow; it is able to judge the thoughts and intentions of the heart. And before him no creature is hidden, but all are naked and laid bare to the eyes of the one to whom we must render an account. Since, then, we have a great high priest who has passed through the heavens, Jesus, the Son of God, let us hold fast to our confession. For we do not have a high priest who is unable to sympathize with our weakness, but we have one who in every respect has been tested as we are, yet without sin. Let us therefore approach the throne of grace with boldness, so that we may receive mercy and find grace to help in time of need.

We have here, in these few but densely packed words, both the greatest of challenges and the greatest of encouragements. Our Lord Jesus is *both* our perfect, righteous judge—whom we cannot fool, cannot bribe—to whom "we must render account," *and also* our "great high priest"—who sympathizes with our weaknesses, ministers as our Advocate at the very throne of heaven—and who, as the letter later assures us, is willing "and able for all time to save those who approach God through him, since he always lives to make intercession for them" (7:25).

This "both and" is essential.

Forget the first—that Jesus is our righteous judge—and we end up with only a sentimentalized spirituality. Such a thing is increasingly popular, these days: popular but also utterly dispensable.

But forget the second—that Jesus is our merciful and gracious high priest, willing and able to save—and we end up with a despairing religion that just leaves us to our own inadequate devices.

Both. And. The dynamic space between these two is life-giving—and for real. Because the One who gives this space—we might also say, who *is* this space—is himself, personally, for real and alive. Notice that throughout today's text, our Lord is spoken of *in the present tense*. He is "living and active." Christ *is* our great high priest—the eternal Son and Word who became our brother, who offered himself, "once for all" (10:10) as the "full, perfect, and sufficient Sacrifice" for sin[1]—and who is able to save all those whom he thereby made his brothers and sisters: including you and me; right here, right now.

This emphasis is one of the great gifts in the Letter to the Hebrews. Jesus is "the same yesterday and today and forever" (13:8). However he is not merely a figure confined to the past, who might have left an inspiring "legacy" but that's it. Rather, he now "always lives"—and by the power of the Holy Spirit, is personally at work in our here-and-now. What a difference this awareness makes! When we say, "He is risen," we mean it. Not merely as an over-vivid metaphor. Rather: Christ—who for our redemption, offered himself to death on the cross—this Christ is truly risen. Enthroned, alive, acting.

And, therefore, for us, he is—he must be—the enduring subject of our theological sentence. My own interests in language—heightened, perhaps, by claiming my option at this point of life, occasionally to be just a bit of a curmudgeon—lead me to pay particular notice to *grammar*.

In any case, I think that we'd all do well to pay more attention to the grammar of faith. How often, in even our pious speaking, is God the *subject* of our sentences? If you'll indulge me speaking in technical terms: we seem to be happy to put God in the genitive, dative, and accusative cases. But how often do we find him in our *nominative*? But to the point: how often, in our thinking, do we apprehend God as the prime act-or in our great pilgrimage?[2]

---

1. Eucharistic Prayer I, in *Book of Common Prayer*, 334.
2. See Rutledge, *By the Word Worked*, 24–25.

What are we, then, to do? As we heard today, Hebrews, itself, gives its two-part answer.

First: "Let us [therefore] hold fast to our confession" (4:14). A key theme of this letter. And this doesn't mean that we just keep repeating, in our mix of things, certain religious formulas. Rather, to "hold fast to our confession" involves our actual life priorities. It commits our deepest allegiance—which then qualifies, governs, orders, and guides all other loyalties that we may have.

Today's Gospel sheds penetrating light on this very thing. Let's hear a portion of it once more:

> Jesus said to them, "Children, how hard it is to enter the kingdom of God! It is easier for a camel to go through the eye of a needle than for someone who is rich to enter the kingdom of God." They were greatly astounded and said to one another, "Then who can be saved?" Jesus looked at them and said, "For mortals it is impossible, but not for God; for God all things are possible." (Mark 10:24b-27)

While this Gospel passage certainly does address our relationship with money, it also speaks to our entire systems of valuation, of *all* sorts. Our Lord's teaching here is further clarified by considering his words in Matthew's Gospel, in the Sermon on the Mount:

> "No one can serve two masters; for a slave will either hate the one and love the other, or be devoted to the one and despise the other. You cannot serve God and wealth." (6:25)

And "wealth" comes in many forms, not just monetary. It can be anything that we value and in which we invest ourselves. Not that valuing something is bad. Of course not. How could we give thanks for anything if we didn't value it? And investing—involving—ourselves in what we value is a part of life's project. The problem starts with making these things our "masters," when they become—practically—rivals to the unique allegiance we owe to God. We start with owning stuff and end up being owned *by* our stuff.

We can make an idol out of anything. Not just the obviously unworthy or degraded things but sometimes, more dangerously, those things that we deem the "best," the most necessary—even the most righteous causes. "The ends justify the means," the world says. The tempter said to Jesus, "All these will I give you, if you will fall down and worship me." Of course, Jesus held fast. "Away with you, Satan! For it is written, 'Worship the Lord your God, and serve only him'" (Matt 4:9–10; Deut 6:13).

But we, facing the same tempting "con," haven't done so well, have we? Just take a look at the spirit of fanaticism that's popping up all along the political spectrum these days: social "enemies," implacably at odds, but growing more and more like each other than they could ever stand to admit.

> "It is easier for a camel to go through the eye of a needle than for someone who is rich to enter the kingdom of God . . . Who then can be saved?"

The answer to that question is hard. Simple but hard. By human power, and even our best aspirations: no one. None. Not by our effort or earning. But, amazingly, by the grace of "God our Savior, who desires that all be saved and come to the knowledge of the truth" (1 Tim 2:4): yes, even the likes of us.

> "Who can be saved?" Jesus looked at them and said, "For mortals it is impossible, but not for God; for God, all things are possible."

We can belong to God's realm—we can "hold fast to our confession"—because *he* has been—and will be—faithful himself. In response to all that God, in Christ, has done and *is* doing, what are *we* then to do? Especially when we fall short—as we will.

Back to Hebrews, once again, for the *second* part of its answer to that very question:

> Let us therefore approach the throne of grace with boldness, so that we may receive mercy and find grace to help in time of need. (4:16)

The Righteous Judge is also our Perfect Advocate. We may trust his goodwill: his understanding, competence, determination—and love. Remember, he is not confined to the past. "Not as orphans are we left," with our only access to him, now, being memories of one who is gone. No. He is "living and active." He knows what he is doing—and he knows exactly what he is dealing with. He is "sharper than any two-edged sword," piercing through all layers of pretense, "able to judge the thoughts and intentions of the heart," (4:12) to whom—nevertheless—"the sinful" may "flee . . . from day to day: Intercessor, Redeemer, great High Priest."[3]

---

3. William Chatterton, "Alleluia! Sing to Jesus," in *Hymnal 1982*, #460.

So, "approach the throne of grace." We're not left to our own devices. In Christ's own high priestly sacrifice, we've been freed from the slavery to all our "stuff." In Christ's own holding fast, we ourselves may begin to keep faith—and also find ample provision for when we fall short, as we certainly will. In our present pilgrimage, we are often slow learners, much in need of remedial lessons in the grammar of faith.

But Jesus Christ will see this long endeavor through. Whatever it takes. Therefore look to him. In all places, in all times and circumstances, look to him, "the pioneer and perfecter of our faith" (12:2). Look to him and draw near.

> "But Lord, are you *sure*? I'm not worthy. I'm not prepared. I don't think I'm making enough progress."
> "Peace, dear one. Approach the throne."

"And He Must Win the Battle"
Christ Church, Kalispell, Montana

First Sunday in Lent, Year C: Rom 10:8b-13 and Luke 4:1–13
March 6, 2022

LENT CERTAINLY IS A season of some deliberate starkness. But at the heart of it, it's not about privation as such. Rather, what it's really to be about is a refreshed discovery of our true abundance. It's to this that the starkness, and all the disciplines of this season, are meant to lead. So how apt it is today, on the first Sunday of Lent, to hear a Gospel account of the temptation of Jesus during his forty days in the wilderness: this critical time of fasting, prayer, and confrontation, before he began his ministry. This episode has much from which we are to learn: about him, and about us.

> For we do not have a high priest who is unable to sympathize with our weaknesses, but we have one who in every respect has been tested as we are, yet without sin. (Heb 4:15)

I invite us to take a look at the series of temptations that our Lord faced, to learn of his victory over them and to know more fully what we ourselves are up against—and to know, even more fully, of *his* victory, that so graciously, and by faith, may be ours as well.

If we look at this set of three temptations, maybe they don't, at first impression, seem so obviously unworthy. No, they're rather more subtle—and insidious—than that. They even might seem rather reasonable, even necessary.

> Jesus, full of the Holy Spirit, returned from the Jordan and was led by the Spirit in the wilderness, where for forty days he was tempted by the devil. He ate nothing at all during those days, and when they were over, he was famished. The devil said to him, "If

> you are the Son of God, command this stone to become a loaf of bread." (4:1–3)

You have such great "personal needs" right now—and you have so much "valuable" work to do. And maybe God hasn't been entirely reasonable in making sure that you're taken care of? So, let me provide the way you can get those needs met. Perhaps just this once.

> Jesus answered him, "It is written, 'One does not live by bread alone.'" Then the devil led him up and showed him in an instant all the kingdoms of the world. And the devil said to him, "To you I will give their glory and all this authority; for it has been given over to me, and I give it to anyone I please. If you, then, will worship me, it will all be yours." (4:4–7; Deut 8:3)

You have such an important cause. And perhaps the means that God gave you to accomplish it just aren't enough to ensure success? So, why not take up my way of getting the job done? After all, my track record seems so much better that his, in terms of getting "my will be done, on earth," doesn't it? I'm feeling generous today. Go ahead, use my own tools against me. Think of all the good you could do with those tools: all the wrongs you could make right. Your cause is important, isn't it? Look at all this fleshly power—my kind of power. If you will worship me, it will all be yours.

> Jesus answered him, "It is written, 'Worship the Lord your God, and serve only him.'" Then the devil took him to Jerusalem, and placed him on the pinnacle of the temple, saying to him, "If you are the Son of God, throw yourself down from here, for it is written, 'He will command his angels concerning you, to protect you,' and 'On their hands they will bear you up, so that you will not dash your foot against a stone.'" (4:8–11; Deut 6:13, Ps 91:11–12)

It's right here from your own Scriptures: an ironclad guarantee. Why not use that guarantee to do something really spectacular? Yes, I know that you have a few "miracles" in mind. Impressive, too, in their own limited way. But they still would be ambiguous signs. You need a wow factor. Why not use my tools of coercion and manipulation? You're missing the mark if you're leaving them any room to think anything else than the thoughts you want them to think. If you really want to close to deal with this rabble, you have to compel their belief. Why settle for a few willing servants when you can get them all as captured slaves? It's for their own good, after all. Engaging with the likes of them personally is just too much of a gamble.

"And He Must Win the Battle"

Jesus answered him, "It is said, 'Do not put the Lord your God to the test.'" (4:12; Deut 6:16)

Jesus prevails where we have failed. He was "tested as we are, yet without sin." Yet amazingly and graciously, his victory—a victory that will continue throughout his ministry—a victory that reaches its culmination on the cross itself—a victory that will be utterly vindicated before the empty tomb on Easter—this victory will be shared with *us*; we who have failed, who have been defeated. By faith, his victory becomes ours.

The Lord is our righteousness. (Jer 23:6)

Christ's victory becomes ours, first by our belonging to him in faith. This first "becoming" is sheer gift: unwarranted, undeserved, unmerited. Once for all.

As we heard in today's lesson from Paul's Letter to the Romans,

> If you confess with your lips that Jesus is Lord and believe in your heart that God raised him from the dead, you will be saved. For one believes with the heart and so is justified, and one confesses with the mouth and so is saved. The scripture says, "No one who believes in him will be put to shame." (10:9–10)

But there's a second phase of this "becoming" which necessarily follows from the first, in which Christ's victory *continues* to become ours—but this time involving our own personal growth into faithful *character*. And this second phase is very much an ongoing process. Usually, for most of us, it's not only gradual but often incremental. Sometimes, frustratingly so. It certainly calls forth all our cooperative effort, but it's grace-powered all the way.

Later, we'll be closing our service today with the hymn "A Mighty Fortress Is Our God." One of my favorites. It's by Martin Luther, based on Psalm 46. Hymn 688 in our hymnal. I thought that I'd share some of its words now, ahead of time, as they are most fitting for all we're considering. You might open your hymnals as I do and follow along if you wish. Verses two and three:

> Did we in our own strength confide, our striving would be losing;
> Were not the right Man on our side, the Man of God's own choosing.
> Dost ask who that may be? Christ Jesus, it is he;
> Lord Sabaoth is his name, from age to age the same,
> And He must win the battle.

And though this world, with devils filled, should threaten to undo us,
We will not fear, for God hath willed His truth to triumph through us.
The prince of darkness grim, we tremble not for him;
His rage we can endure, for lo! his doom is sure,
One little word shall fell him.

Wonderful!

But I invite you to ask, what is the "one little word" that shall fell the prince of darkness? What do you think? There might a number of possibilities. But there's strong evidence that the "one little word" that Luther had in mind was this: "liar." The prince of darkness "is a liar and the father of lies" (John 8:44). The devil is a *liar* and makes alternating lying appeals both to our grandiosity and to our despair. But they are a fraud and a con. Let's make a point of remembering that.

But our great Savior and gracious Lord is trustworthiness himself. Jesus Christ is always the amen, the faithful and true—no matter what! (Rev 3:14; 19:11). He is "the right man on our side . . . and he must win the battle." In him, we abide in the "life that really is life" (1 Tim 6:19).

And in a world all too enthralled with miserable substitutes, that's exactly why Christ came: that we "may have life, and have it abundantly" (John 10:10).

"The Banquet of Consequence"
Christ Church, Kalispell, Montana

Proper 9, Year C: Gal 6:7–16 and Luke 9:51–62
Sunday, July 3, 2022

> Do not be deceived; God is not mocked, for you reap whatever you sow. If you sow to your own flesh, you will reap corruption from the flesh; but if you sow to the Spirit, you will reap eternal life from the Spirit. (6:7–8)

SO WE WERE JUST given to hear today from Paul's Letter to the Galatians. It's from the very end of the epistle. To appreciate it fully, it will help if we bring to mind what's come before. Here's what we heard in last week's portion:

> You were called to freedom, brothers and sisters; only do not use your freedom as an opportunity for self-indulgence, but through love become servants of one another. For the whole law is summed up in a single commandment, "You shall love your neighbor as yourself." If, however, you bite and devour one another, take care that you are not consumed by one another. Live by the Spirit, I say, and do not gratify the desires of the flesh. For what the flesh desires is opposed to the Spirit, and what the Spirit desires is opposed to the flesh; for these are opposed to each other. (5:13–17)

Remember that "flesh," as Paul uses the word, does not mean the physical, the material. Rather, "flesh" means human life lived as though we were our own invention, driven by the pursuit of what we think we want, without God. It is a "way of being"—in fact, a way of *decreasing* being—at odds with itself and also at odds with the Spirit of God.

We're certainly still a mix in this present life. We're still in a long pilgrimage that's far from being one continuous chain of pious success stories. But ultimately, as a governing principle, it's one or the other: flesh or Spirit.

Here, again, from last week's portion:

> The fruit of the Spirit is love, joy, peace, patience, kindness, generosity, faithfulness, gentleness, and self-control . . . And those who belong to Christ Jesus have crucified the flesh with its passions and desires. If we live by the Spirit, let us also be guided by the Spirit. (5:22–23b,24–25)

I cannot stress enough that the way of the Spirit and the call to bear the fruit of the Spirit are not only for when times are good and things are going our way! They are to be the ongoing characteristic of the people of Jesus Christ in all conditions, in all circumstances: in the good and the bad; the painful and the joyful, in the frustrating and the fulfilling, in winning and in losing,

> The fruit of the Spirit is love, joy, peace, patience, kindness, generosity, faithfulness, gentleness, and self-control.

Having trouble with it? Of course. We all do from time to time. What then? As always: repent, remember, seek, and ask! And if need be, pray for the courage to be vulnerable to growing into a new disposition, new habits of being. As Paul wrote in another letter, to the Philippians:

> Work out your own salvation with fear and trembling; for it is God who is at work in you, enabling you both to will and to work for his good pleasure. (2:12b-13)

Now back to the verses from today's lesson:

> Do not be deceived; God is not mocked, for you reap whatever you sow. If you sow to your own flesh, you will reap corruption from the flesh; but if you sow to the Spirit, you will reap eternal life from the Spirit. (6:7–8)

Indeed: we reap what we sow. There's a telling saying attributed to Robert Lewis Stevenson: "Sooner or later everyone sits down to a banquet of consequences." I would add: either the consequences of making idols of all our stuff (even the best of it) or the very different consequences of trusting the renewing grace of God—a grace specifically offered to the unworthy and undeserving, a grace that justifies through faith in Christ and

"The Banquet of Consequence"

then reforms by the power of the Spirit. And yes, this means growing into different sorts of people. "New creation" (6:15).

Among other things, this means deliverance from a life governed by our passions. By "passions" what is meant is unrestrained fleshly devotion to all that we think we know, all that we think we feel, and all that we think we want. I know that this sense of the word "passion" may seem somewhat antique. Nowadays, "passions" seem to be thought an unquestionable good. In present day job interviews, for example, we may be asked, "What's your passion?" But in older use of the word, it often had a rather negative connotation—and I think, rightly so. Because a life utterly governed by our passions (even those we think most right and necessary) is a captive life. And in response all temptation to return to captivities, we need to heed Paul's urgent appeal:

> For freedom Christ has set us free. Stand firm, therefore, and do not submit again to a yoke of slavery. (5:1)

External realities do matter, for us and for everyone. Of course. Yet the worst captivities are those we carry *within* us. And the greatest, most enduring freedom is, likewise, interior. To be governed by passions is to be less alive, not more; less present, not more so.

Please be assured that we are not meant to be apathetic people—detached, uncaring. By no means! We are certainly meant to be deeply concerned, truly involved, here and now, and active for the repair of the world. We are meant to feel deeply and compassionately—and rejoice in all that is good. However, either intemperate cheering or intemperate wailing about the affairs of this present life is an all-too-likely sign of "sowing to the flesh."

There's a quote from the eighteenth-century English statesman Edmund Burke that I especially like:

> It is ordained in the eternal constitution of things, that men of intemperate minds cannot be free. Their passions forge their fetters.[1]

In marked contrast with all such fettered mindsets, we are to "rejoice that our names are written in heaven" (Luke 10:20). Furthermore, I'm convinced that it is specifically in our heavenly-mindedness that we are able make a real difference for the good in this present world.

Our present culture conspires to keep everyone in constant states of anger, anxiety, and agitation. The hardened edges on both sides of the

---

1. "Letter to a Member of the National Assembly," in Burke, *Reflections on the Revolution*, 680.

political spectrum spend half the time in sneering, contemptuous dismissal of large portions of the population—and then, the other half of the time, howling their turns of loss—and the consequences of loss. We were clearly told—were we not?—that "your anger does not produce God's righteousness" (Jas 1:20). But culturally speaking, we keep on thinking that it can.

There must be a better way. Thanks be, in the gift of God, there is. The active presence, in our country, of a people with a different life disposition—and with another kind of cultural deportment—might just make a life-saving difference. I'm not saying that we Christians are the end-all-and-be-all, or that we can fix everything all by ourselves. But I am confident that the people of Jesus Christ, faithfully "sowing to the Spirit," in addition to their greatest blessing of "reaping to eternal life," just might also, in this our present time, be a key part of making it possible—in the words of Abraham Lincoln—

> that government of the people, by the people, and for the people"
> might not perish from the earth.[2]

We would do very well, as Christians, to ponder such a call—and such an aspiration—as we celebrate our country's Independence Day.

Meanwhile, dear ones, here now—on this Lord's Day and in this place—we are gathered in a radically new banquet of consequence. Not the consequences of our just deserts, but the astounding consequence of God's gracious mercy: real, undiminishing life in the body and blood of him who came to save sinners and make all things new.

---

2. "Address at Gettysburg", November 19, 1863, in Lincoln, *Speeches and Writings*, 536.

"Blessed Is the Man"

Church of the Incarnation, Great Falls, Montana

Year C, Proper 18: Ps 1, Deut 30:15–20, and Luke 14:25–33
September 4, 2022

> Now large crowds were traveling with Jesus; and he turned and said to them, "Whoever comes to me and does not hate father and mother, wife and children, brothers and sisters, yes, and even his own life, cannot be my disciple." (Luke 14:25–26)

So we hear in today's gospel passage. Surely this is one of the many "now *wait* a moment!" occasions that come to us when reading or listening to the Holy Scriptures. What did *you* think (or feel) when you heard it just now?

It's a "hard saying"—that's for sure. Let's start with making clear what it *cannot* mean. If we read the Scriptures as a whole, it's undeniable that we are *not* literally to hate, despise, or hold in contempt our parents, spouses, siblings, or our own lives. Rather, we are to hold all of these in respect, honor, and—yes—even love.

What is our Lord talking about, then?

His words, here, are—quite evidently—*hyperbole*. As we know, a hyperbole is a very heightened exaggeration that communicates a point. We'd certainly be well-cautioned against ready-to-go dismissals of our Lord's hard teachings, in general, just by telling ourselves, "Well, he was *exaggerating*." But in this saying, in particular, it's fully evident that hyperbole is the figure of speech that he was using.

In the point at hand, "hate" means to place in a *lower priority*, to put lower down in the scale of our loyalties. "Hate" here means that we love something else (or someone else) *more*. This is what Jesus is telling us, precisely in a manner that seizes our attention—in a manner that we cannot evade.

What greatly sharpens the point is that Jesus is saying this not about obviously unworthy things—not about the stuff that we already know that we have to get rid of if we want to be his disciples—but rather, about things that otherwise would be our highest, most sacred priorities!

So then, what is it (or rather, who is it) that we are truly to love *more*? Obviously: God. And our share in God's kingdom is to be *more* important than all else that we would otherwise deem "most important."

Of course, we all have our ways of evading the obvious. And that's why Jesus spoke to us in the way that he did. But by no means are we to think that he's advocating some sort of joyless, miserable existence. Here's the saving paradox of the gospel: it is specifically—in fact, it is *only*—the cross-bearing life that is the blessed life.

Through the Cross joy has come into all the world.[1]

Astoundingly, the Christian proclamation is that the blessed life—our truly *happy* life—comes only in our ongoing union with the cross of Jesus Christ. This is the only way to resurrection: through his cross. No detours, no alternate path. "The gate is narrow and the road is hard that leads to life" (Matt 7:14; see also Luke 13:24).

We aren't to think, however, that this is because God is stingy or desires to be harsh. It's just the truth about the reality in which we find ourselves. But we can enter that gate—we can take that road—because Jesus has already done so on our behalf. In him, God was "first in line" in the way of the cross. And his cross accomplishes what our own best sacrificial endeavors, in themselves, never could.

In John's Gospel, the last words of Christ on that cross were "it is finished." In other words, "it is accomplished" (19:30). Not merely "it is made possible"—not just "I've given you the best possible head start"—but, precisely, "it is accomplished."

This is why the same Lord who gives us such hard words as we hear today, also says:

> "Come to me, all you that are weary and are carrying heavy burdens, and I will give you rest. Take my yoke upon you, and learn

---

1. "Having Beheld the Resurrection of Christ," *Resurrection Matins*, Byzantine Rite, in Hapgood, *Service Book*, 31; also Anthem 1, the Liturgy of Good Friday, in *Book of Common Prayer*, 281.

"Blessed Is the Man"

from me; for I am gentle and humble in heart, and you will find rest for your souls. For my yoke is easy, and my burden is light." (Matt 11:28–30)

But this doesn't mean that we're to be the passive consumers of spiritual benefits. We are to take his yoke upon us and learn from him—to the uttermost. Indeed, as he said,

"Whoever does not carry the cross and follow me cannot be my disciple." (Luke 14:27)

That sounds demanding—and it is. What about that easy yoke and that light burden? This is a paradoxical combination for us. But by contrast, it's infinitely easier and lighter than what we've been trying to pull off on our own, without him.

The way of Jesus Christ—in both its astounding gift and also its uncompromising demand—is the way to the blessed, truly happy life.

Today's appointed psalm—Psalm 1—likewise devotes its attention to just what makes for real happiness. Let's spend some time with it. This morning, we're using a different translation[2] that preserves some important features of the Hebrew original that our more commonly used renderings miss. Here it is again:

> How happy is the one who does not walk in the counsel of the wicked,
> nor follow the path that sinners tread,
> nor take seat in the company of scoffers;
> but who delights in the Law of the Lord,
> and on that Law meditates day and night!

> Such a one will be like a tree planted by the rivers of water,
> that bears fruit in its season—
> and prospers in all doings.

> Not so the wicked; not so!
> They are like the chaff that the wind drives away.
> They will not stand firm when judgement comes;
> nor sinners in the assembly of the righteous.

> For the Lord watches over the way of the righteous;
> but the way of the wicked is doomed.

---

2. My own, from the Hebrew, checking with the Septuagint Greek, and in consideration of the renderings in the Revised English Bible, the New Jerusalem Bible, and the New International Version (2011).

One of the first things to be noticed in the psalm is the striking shift from the *singular* to the *plural*—from the godly *one* "who delights in the Law of the Lord," "who is like a tree planted by the rivers of water," to the ungodly many: "*They* are like the chaff that the wind drives away." This shift is underscored in the text and is very deliberate.

Unfortunately, it's this very thing that is disguised in the versions with which we are more familiar. Why so? It was for the understandable good intention of avoiding undue masculinization of the message. That's why we went from "blessed is *the man*" to such things as "happy are *they*."

We should note, however, that in the Hebrew original, oddly enough, the word is specifically '*ish*—"man" in the sense of a male—rather than '*adam*—human in the general sense. So while it is perhaps better now avoided because of the likely misunderstandings, "blessed"—or "how happy"—"is *the man*" wasn't such a bad translation after all.

But the point at hand, is that the godly *one*—even if seemingly standing alone—is more truly happy than those who've given into all this world's versions of ungodly peer pressure. The lonely tree in our psalm, planted by the rivers of water, is not only alive but flourishing. The cloud of chaff, on the other hand, is just many bits of stuff, once alive but now dead. It may seem like a great company—quite a "community"—but that's only an illusion. The "bits" no longer have any real connection with each other.

The second thing we notice in the psalm is that in the description of the truly happy life, what's mentioned first are the options which are *declined*—the things which are *not* done.

> How happy is the one who does not walk in the counsel of the wicked,
> nor follow the path that sinners tread,
> nor take seat in the company of scoffers.

It may seem a little strange, so upfront, to stress what we *don't* do in a godly life. But this is a stress we find many times throughout the Scriptures. The series of "nots" in the Ten Commandments comes to mind:

> You shall *not* have other gods; you shall *not* make idols, shall *not* worship them, *not* bow down to them; shall *not* make wrongful use of the name of the Lord your God; shall *not* murder; *not* commit adultery; *not* steal; *not* bear false witness; *not* covet. (Exod 20:1–17)

Of course, we'd prefer a "spirituality" which told us that all we needed was to be "affirmed" and given permission to be our own "authentic selves"—whatever *that* means. But the Holy Spirit gives us what we *need*, not what we'd prefer.

Our reading from Deuteronomy has some severe warnings in it, along with its promises, and of course, as we've been considering, today's Gospel is quite strong on the negatives too. And if we try to tell ourselves that our Lord was just having some sort of "bad day," I'd suggest looking pretty much anywhere else in Matthew, Mark, Luke, or John. The Sermon on the Mount—Matthew, chapters five through seven—for example, is loaded with its own extensive series of "nots."

The mercy of God gives us what we need, not what we think we want. Real love, as opposed to its sentimentalized reduction, is sometimes "tough love." Living into a godly life is certainly a *response* to what God has done. But that response *does* include recognizing the fact that there are many "options" which for us, now, are *no longer* to be options. We come to know, in the mercy of God, that real happiness is not just "having fun." Nor it is "getting our way." Nor is it to be found in desperately trying to manipulate our exterior circumstances so that these might somehow "make" us happy.

Real happiness is an *interior disposition*: the disposition of one who lives in (and by) the Passover of the Lord—the disposition of one now able to "delight in the Lord's Instruction" and therefore immersed in that instruction "day and night." Of course, this doesn't mean that we're now living in complete, sinless perfection! But we *are* in an ongoing, serious progress in "beholding what we are" and "becoming what we have received" in Christ.[3]

This not only involves a renouncing that which is manifestly sinful and unworthy, although that's most certainly part of it. We are *also* summoned to say "no" to making the *better* things into *rivals* to God. That's often the more difficult temptation we deal with. Subsidiary goods that we make rivals to our one ultimate good, are still *idols*.

"You shall not have other gods besides me." And the sad truth is that which we *idolize* we must *lose*. Even our own selves.

When we seek from anything (or anyone) else what only can God can give, we are setting the stage for great injury and colossal disappointment—both for ourselves and for others. So whatever it is, from out-and-out wickedness, all the way to the things we deem the best, we must take care to heed the Lord's call: "Christian, love me *more*."[4]

---

3. See Augustine, *Essential Sermons* 272 (Hill, 318).

4. Cecil Frances Alexander, "Jesus Calls Us; O'er the Tumult," verse 3, in *Hymnal 1982*, #550.

Here's yet another one of those great gospel paradoxes: it is only when we can stand to be *one* with the Lord that we find real community, living connection—indeed, the great assembly constituted in his righteousness.

Did we in our own strength confide, our striving would be losing.[5]

It is in strength of Jesus Christ—it is in *his* accomplishment—that we undertake our own Pilgrim's Progress. It is *he*, the eternal Son of God, incarnate, who is the Blessed Man. It is he, crucified and risen, who is the Font and Giver of all our blessedness—and the One in whom we will find what it is to be truly happy.

---

5. Martin Luther, "A Mighty Fortress Is Our God," verse 2, in *Hymnal 1982*, #688.

"God Is Reigning from the Tree"

Church of the Incarnation, Great Falls, Montana

The Last Sunday after Pentecost, Year C: Col 1:11–20
and Luke 23:33–43
November 20, 2022

> The royal banners forward go ... Fulfilled is all that David told in true prophetic song of old ... for God is reigning from the tree.[1]

TODAY, THE LAST SUNDAY after Pentecost—the Last Sunday before we begin a new worship year—is devoted to the theme of the kingship of Christ. It is highly significant that as we do so, we have been given to hear the account, in Luke's Gospel, of the crucifixion.

As we behold the cross of Jesus—without evasion, without all the distancing mechanisms with which we seek to shield ourselves—we are beholding *reality*: the truth about ourselves and the prior and greater truth about God. This is both terrible and wondrous.

Ultimate reality *is*—by definition—the kingdom of Jesus Christ. In varying degrees, all sorts of things are "real" or "true." But Christ's kingdom is always *more* true, *more* real than all else, no matter what. This is what our ongoing growth in faith enables to see and to know, more and more.

But to perceive that kingdom is—in one aspect—terrible for us, because it perfectly reveals God's righteous judgement against all sin. And this most certainly includes our sin—*ours*—not just the stuff that those bad "others" (however we define them) do.

The cross banishes all "selective outrage." It banishes all the self-congratulation that masquerades as "prophetic preaching." The crucifixion of

---

1. Venantius Honorius Fortunatus, *Hymnal 1982*, #162.

Jesus is itself a revelation of the last judgment. We don't need to wait for "the end of time" to hear the word that—humanly speaking—is impossible for us to bear.

But, in faith, to see the kingdom of the Crucified is wondrous as well. Because in it, our salvation is also revealed. However, the word "also" here might possibly be misleading. Because salvation is not an "add-on," not a secondary reality, not a "Plan B" over against judgment. Rather, judgment and salvation are two aspects of the same divine action. We, the people of Christ before his cross, are—at the same time—perfectly judged *and* perfectly saved.

> [God] has rescued us from the dominion of darkness and brought us into the kingdom of the Son he loves, in whom we have redemption, the forgiveness of sins . . . For God was pleased to have all his fullness dwell in him, and through him to reconcile to himself all things, whether things on earth or things in heaven, by making peace through his blood, shed on his Cross. (Col 1:13, 19–20)

Therefore: the cross is not something that God the Father simply "did" *to* Jesus. Rather, on Calvary—in Christ's self-offering—God's own sacrificial, saving love was acting *for* us: for *us*, who, right there, were revealed to be unworthy and undeserving.

The eyes of faith enable us to perceive what the eyes of flesh cannot. Christ came into his kingdom, right then and there, on the cross. And by grace, we get to be a part of his kingdom: we, the very ones "who set at nought and sold him, pierced, and nailed him to the tree."

Terrible. Wondrous.

Charles Wesley's hymn "Lo! He Comes with Clouds Descending"[2] is very fittingly paired with today's epistle and Gospel readings.

The hymn speaks of those "deeply wailing," as they "the true Messiah see," and also those who "with what rapture, gaze on his glorious scars"— "those dear tokens of his passion, [that] still his dazzling body bears."

As I ponder these words, I wonder: just who are the "wailing," and who are the "rapturous"? Are they two entirely different sets of people? No, not necessarily. Rather, I am convinced that Christ's people—at least in regard to this present life—are *both*.[3] To be very sure, it is promised to

---

2. *Hymnal 1982*, #57.

3. The crucifixion of Jesus is itself the ultimate apocalyptic event. In it, "ahead" of time—as we now experience it—we are given to see both the end of the world and the last judgment. Matthew's Gospel markedly highlights this (see 27:45, 50–52).

"God Is Reigning from the Tree"

Christ's own that such wailing that indeed is rightfully ours is only for a time and that the *joy* in him begins even now and endures forever. But to try to see the cross on our own terms—determined to continue in our futile self-justifications—forsakes the joy and leaves only the wailing.

Yet—thanks be to God—when we, trusting no claim but that of God's mercy, appeal to our crucified Lord, "Jesus, remember me when you come into your Kingdom" (Luke 23:42), then we may know—"with what rapture"—that "by his wounds we are healed" (Isa 53:5 NIV). My prayer for all of us—for you, for me—is for the grace to *know*, ever more deeply, that there, on his royal cross, he did—so savingly—remember us.

"[Jesus said,] 'And I, when I am lifted up from the earth, will draw all people to myself.' He said this to show the kind of death he was to die" (John 12:32–33). We "were there, when they crucified" him.[4] The time of Jesus—most especially *then*, on the cross—holds *all* times, and his place—most especially *there*—holds all places.

There is more to see of God's victory than only Good Friday. Of course. "Christ has died; Christ is risen; Christ will come again!"[5] But on Calvary that victory was already accomplished: then and there, "from the foundation of the world" (Rev 13:8) and therefore, *also now* and forever.

"Every eye shall now behold him; robed in dreadful majesty." Yes. But for "his ransomed worshippers," it is in this dread vision that we also behold our salvation and peace; our transformation and eternal joy.

"Alleluia! Thou shalt reign"—dear Lord and King—"and thou alone."

The revelation of Christ—the archetypal and ultimate Adam—reveals our present Adam for what he is (and what we are). Were it not for redemptive grace this would be unbearable for us, but in the entirely of faith it must still necessarily be borne—at least for a time. (See Barth's *Christ and Adam*. Barth's discussion of election in *Church Dogmatics* 2/2 is relevant as well (sections 32–35).

4. See #172 in *Hymnal 1982*.

5. The Great Thanksgiving, Prayer A, Memorial Acclamation, in *Book of Common Prayer*, 363

"The Surpassing Value"
All Saints Church, Columbia Falls, Montana

Year A, Proper 22: Exod 20:2-3 and Phil 3:4b-14
Sunday, October 8, 2023

> Whatever gains I had, these I have come to regard as loss because of Christ. More than that, I regard everything as loss because of the surpassing value of Knowing Christ Jesus my Lord. For his sake I have suffered the loss of all things, and I regard them as rubbish, in order that I may gain Christ and be found in him. (Phil 3:7–9a)

FOR ALL SORTS OF reasons, I personally don't do "social media." And I choose to be limited and selective too when it comes to consuming what we call "the news."

But I did hear of some recent trend in which men were asked how often they thought about the Roman Empire, and—supposedly—the results indicated that vast numbers of men think about it very frequently: if not every day, then at least several times a week. However, this seems to me to be highly questionable. It doesn't match up with the men that I know—and, of course, being a man myself, I like to think that I have some accurate idea of what's going on inside of my head.

When most people say "Roman Empire," what they have in mind—and certainly what the recent social media trend references—is the Roman Empire in the West, which fell in the year 476 of our present common era. The power of Ancient Rome was one of the most remarkable success stories—if we may call it that—in the entire record of human civilization. Ancient Rome's story is a story of a thousand years.

(To put that in perspective, we're still almost three years away from the 250th anniversary of the founding of the United States. I hope that we

"The Surpassing Value"

make it.) So I guess that maybe it wouldn't be quite so strange that some men might think of Ancient Rome frequently, especially in times like ours.

But it seems that I think of Ancient Rome less frequently than many others. When I do think of it, especially lately, it more often has been in connection with Saint Augustine of Hippo, one of the greatest fathers of the early church. The last couple of years, in particular, I've been delving into one of Augustine's greatest works: *The City of God*. Not a light read but very much worth it. One of the things that strikes me, as I do so, was how quickly that empire—how quickly that long-term human success story—came crashing down.

When Augustine was a young man, while the empire was no longer at its heyday, he still enjoyed its considerable benefits and its still-remarkable functionality. As an older man, he lived to hear of the Sack of Rome in the year 410 by the Visigoths, which inspired him to begin work writing *The City of God*. What had happened in the catastrophe? Was it really true that Christians were at fault? How were Christians to make sense of the sudden decay of all the earthly securities they had known?

He took a long, deep look at all these questions. And later, while he was dying, the Vandals were ravaging the remnants of Roman civilization where he lived in North Africa, holding his own city in siege. He died in the year 430. The bits and pieces of what was left of the empire in the West didn't last much longer. I find it sobering and chilling to consider how fast things can fall apart in human societies.

In *The City of God*, Augustine looked at "the big picture" in considerable depth, but he also did so with practical relevance at the personal level—apt for those he was addressing in his "then" but also enduringly apt for people like us now. I'm not saying that Augustine was perfect or always right. (There's only One who is perfect and always right. All the rest of us are works in progress.) But God also—astoundingly—gifts us through one another.

In faith "we are surrounded by so great a cloud of witnesses" (Heb 12:1): a great company through the centuries, of brothers, sisters, fathers, and mothers, with whom we are taught, nourished, challenged, and inspired. Yes, it can be a little messy and confusing. (And sometimes, more than just "a little.") Yet, in my repeated observation, "throw it all out and start from scratch" attitudes always result in massive—and usually destructive—trade-downs. *The City of God* runs for about a thousand pages. But for now, there's just one short phrase from it that I'd like to share with you. Here it is:

> As it seems to me, a brief and true definition of virtue is "rightly ordered love."[1]

"Rightly ordered love." However, the crisis of the human condition, alienated from God, is that we are *disordered*—and disordered to an extent beyond all well-intentioned endeavors of our own to "fix." "Just trusting our hearts," just trusting ourselves, won't do it.

In the words of the prophet Jeremiah, "The heart is devious above all else; it is perverse—who can understand it?" (17:9) And centuries later, a much noted Christian theologian—drawing on both much introspection and much observation—wrote that our "nature, so to speak, is a perpetual factory of idols."[2]

Drawing on our own "potential," such as it is, drawing on even the best of our resources "within," we find that we cannot even keep the first of the Ten Commandments:

> I am the Lord your God, who brought you out of the land of Egypt, out of the house of slavery; you shall have no other gods before me. (Exod 20:2–3)
>
> *You shall have no other gods before me.*

We may tell ourselves that of course we have "no other gods before" him. But I can tell you, from both long personal and pastoral experience, that this easy self-assurance often requires a second, and deeper, look.

Our reordering requires a saving intervention from beyond ourselves. The good news is that God indeed—in, through, and by his Son, Jesus Christ—*has* so savingly intervened! Only in that intervention is the unbridgeable gap closed, the old made new, the impossible brought to pass. The Surpassing Value has broken through to us, and only in our encounter with it—*or rather, with him*—are we able to see the idols for what they are, and let them go. Only by this, do we begin to enter the life of what Augustine called "rightly ordered love." We didn't figure it out.

Rather, the surpassing value himself—in amazing, unmerited, undeserved grace—somehow valued *us*, "to the point of death—even death on a Cross" (Phil 2:8b). Saint Paul, in today's second lesson, from the Letter to

---

1. Augustine, *City of God* 15.22 (Bettenson, 637).
2. Calvin, *Institutes* 1.11.8 (Battles, 108).

the Philippians, gives powerful testimony to an astoundingly reordered life. Once again,

> Whatever gains I had, these I have come to regard as loss because of Christ. More than that, I regard everything as loss because of the surpassing value of knowing Christ Jesus my Lord. For his sake I have suffered the loss of all things, and I regard them as rubbish, in order that I may gain Christ and be found in him, not having a righteousness of my own . . . but one that comes through faith in Christ, the righteousness from God based on faith. (3:7–9)

I ought to let you know that the word "rubbish" in the phrase "I regard them as rubbish" is a far-too-polite rendition of what the original Greek says.

But frankly, we can find the concept of a reordered life both frightening and uncongenial. Across the board on the contemporary American religious scene is the idea that the "job" of spirituality is to make us feel good about ourselves.

Affirmed, applauded, "purred at" for just about everything—bring it on! But to be truly inspired, challenged in our ongoing growth in the reordered life, with the real Christ at the center—about that sort of thing we may not be nearly so sure, if at all.

The idea of a Christ who might call us to any significant change, any substantial adjustments in how and what we think; that he might ever call us to leave anything behind—and that in him we have been enfolded in a long-term yet determined process of becoming who we really are—this can be intimidating spiritual territory.

And as God has seen fit—for his own reasons—most often, to play out the process of our Sanctification so very gradually, so very incrementally, we—even as a people of faith—are not yet fully immune to the idolatrous impulse. Not at all.

The most dangerous idols are sometimes not the stuff that we *know* is bad but rather, things we deem to be good that we then put in God's unique place. And we're not even immune to taking what we deem to be the good—whether that's our emotions, our comforts, our strongly held opinions, or our politics—and simply slapping on these the label "Christ."

This is why, on the contemporary American church scene, the various denominations are rapidly becoming wholly owned subsidiaries of this or that sociopolitical affiliation. This is also why much "preaching" in

American churches on hot topics of the day that bills itself on being "prophetic" actually can be an exercise in communal self-congratulation.

"We few, we happy few"[3] are so very thankful that we are "not like other people" (Luke 18:11). How good it can feel to "repent," so earnestly, of *other* people's sins!

The left and the right divide up the denominational spoils, and the church across the board becomes less and less the church. People just get more entrenched in impermeable self-righteousness—more polarized, more and more sure that "otherness" is simply evil.

I see a marked trend of American churches becoming sociopolitical monocultures, less and less able to live with difference. And in sad irony, those congregations which most fervently espouse the noble values of "diversity and inclusion" are usually no exception at all.

I'm not saying that there's no godly place for any convictions, commitments, and action inspired by our best insights: just that these, along with everything else in our lives, must never even come close to being confused for the One Who Is Our Surpassing Value. The surest way to lose anything good in our lives—the fastest way to turn it into toxic rubbish—is to use it as a replacement for God.

> "As it seems to me, a brief and true definition of virtue is 'rightly ordered love.'"

Our getting there, all the way, is a long journey—but it starts *now*. God has intervened! We now belong to the One who is the "Faithful and True" (Rev 19:11); the One who offered perfect obedience; the One who won the battle on our behalf—the One who is, for us, the fount and source of our rightly ordered humanness.

> "I want to know Christ and the power of his resurrection and the sharing of his sufferings by becoming like him in his death." (3:10)

Of course, in our long journey into all this, we won't always get it right. God give us grace to welcome the ongoing process of the right ordering of our love, the process of coming always to perceive—and rejoice in—the surpassing value.

> Not that I have already obtained this or have already reached the goal; but I press on to make it my own, because Christ Jesus has made me his own. Beloved, I do not consider that I have made it

---

3. William Shakespeare, *Henry V*, scene 3, line 60.

"The Surpassing Value"

my own; but this one thing I do: forgetting what lies behind and straining forward to what lies ahead, I press on toward the goal for the prize of the heavenly call of God in Christ Jesus. (3:12–14)

But God has made the people he has brought into this long journey—including you and me, still very much works in progress—a part of his astounding work of the healing and renewal of all things, come what may and in the face of whatever the fleshly appearances of success or failure.

The society in which Augustine lived is gone; the once vibrant church in his corner of the world, vanished, except for few ruins. Yet he was—and is—a citizen of the enduring city (Heb 13:14). And in God's purpose, Augustine's labors on behalf of that city are by no means lost. Indeed, they are still at work; both for us—and by God's grace, God's ongoing gifting in Christ—they are still at work in us, too.

Empires fall; earthly securities dissolve—sometimes much sooner than we might expect or hope, but as Paul wrote at the beginning of the Letter to the Philippians,

> I am confident of this, that the One who began a good work among you will bring it to completion by the Day of Jesus Christ. (1:9)

That's not a bad thing for *all* of us to think about, at least several times a week, if not every day.

"Something Else"
All Saints Church, Columbia Falls, Montana

Third Sunday in Lent, Year A: Rom 4:3–5, 23–25; 5:1–11
and John 4:5–42
March 12, 2023

To paraphrase a recurring line from "Daily Affirmation," a set of Saturday Night Live skits of some years ago: "You're good enough, you're smart enough, and doggone it, people ought to like you!"

The line was funny because we recognized how shallow—really, how contentless—that "affirmation" actually was: feel-good stuff, but that's it.

But I have to say that I find much of contemporary American religion—across the sociopolitical and theological spectrums—often doesn't offer much more. "You're good enough, you're smart enough, and doggone it, people ought to like you!"

The general expectation, more and more, seems to be that it's the job of the churches to make us feel good about ourselves. Of course, that can't be why churches are here. And deep down, we know that it's a shallow expectation, that—even if it's met—is just a quick fix, at best. Deep down, by the grace of God, we don't believe the superficial "affirmations." We know that we need something else.

This morning, in our second scripture lesson, we are given a strong dose of that "something else." Paul's Letter to the Romans. Justification by faith. I would bid us to bind today's words in our memories; to ponder them well, in the coming week—and beyond. They're not entirely easy words—that's for sure!—but I have found them life-giving, and I pray that you will, too.

We could spend far more time than we have now; we could spend days, months—even a lifetime—and still not exhaust this text. My intention, God

"Something Else"

being my helper, is to provide some modest assistance in the process of this reading going to work in us.

> Since we are justified by faith, we have peace with God through our Lord Jesus Christ. (5:1)

Classic words, so central to our faith, that have both provided great comfort and inspired much controversy in the history of the church! We'll be delving, a bit, into some deep theological waters. But I hope that you don't worry about that. At least, not too much. By the merciful grace of God, I believe that you *can* handle the truth![1]

First, *who* is doing the justifying? Not we ourselves—let's get clear on that, from the start. Not even our faith is doing the justifying. No, "it is God who justifies" (Rom 8:33). Faith is the channel through which we take hold of what God has done. Self-justification? Biblically speaking, that's a contradiction in terms. Impossible! Although we certainly have tried, haven't we? But it's a fraud that we perpetrated on ourselves.

Self-justification? It's a delusion. "It is God who justifies."

Second, *what* is justification? To be justified is to be declared righteous—to be acquitted—by the One with the authority to do so. It's not a "process" we undertake but a divine declaration. And it happens not at the end of our life in Christ *but at the beginning* of our life in Christ. This is of critical importance. Don't get me wrong. There's plenty of "process" in our pilgrimage in faith. But not in our justification per se. That's a once-for-all thing; a done deal that then makes possible all that is to follow.

Third, who *are those* who *are* justified? Here we come to the wonder, scandal—the hope and the outrage—of the gospel. Who *are* those whom God has justified? The ungodly, the undeserving, the unprepared, the weak; sinners—those at enmity with God! In other words, people like you and me, the women at the well (John 4:5–42), all of us.

> Since all have sinned and fallen short of the glory of God, they are now justified by his grace as a gift, through the redemption that is in Christ Jesus. (Rom 3:23–24)

Justification of the *ungodly*. Outrageous; wonderful.

> Now to one who works, wages are not reckoned as a gift but as something due. But to one who without works trusts him who

---

1. A riff on the well-known line spoken by the character Colonel Jessep in the film *A Few Good Men*, masterfully played by Jack Nicholson.

> justifies the ungodly, such faith is reckoned as righteousness . . . While we were still weak, at the right time Christ died for the ungodly . . . God proves his love for us in that while we still were sinners Christ died for us . . . For if while we were enemies, we were reconciled to God through the death of his Son, much more surely, having been reconciled, will we be saved by his life. (4:4–5; 5:6, 8, 10)

God acquits—God "reckons" as righteous—those who take hold of his promise given in Jesus Christ. And for God in Christ, there is no such thing as too far or too hard. This promise extends even to the most unlikely—even to the likes of me and of you!

But does the justification of the ungodly mean that God is perpetrating some legal fiction? By no means. Because through the self-offering of Christ—"to the point of death, even death of a cross" (Phil 2:8)—God has *intervened*. In Christ "and him crucified" (1 Cor 2:2), God has accomplished the great exchange: Christ took upon himself "the sin of the world"; he accepted the imputation—upon himself—of "the iniquity of us all" (Isa 53:6). And imputed to those who cleave to this Christ, in faith, are his righteousness—and his active obedience—even to the likes of us. Humanly speaking, impossible! But remember, we are speaking here of what *God* has done: the God "who gives life to the dead and calls into existence the things that do not exist" (Rom 4:17).

To stress, once more: this is not the end result of our Christian faith journey but its very *beginning*. It all starts from here.

This doesn't mean, of course, that we are now simply and passively flopped onto some spiritual conveyor belt all the way to heaven. Growth, challenges, unexpected joys, and transformation—usually incremental but transformation nonetheless—are all part of the long journey in which—more and more—we "become what we have received." But it's not as though we were just once zapped clean and then left to slog it out on our own. This journey is grace-fueled all the way.

Words of the Lady Julian of Norwich come to mind:

> Would you know what your Lord meant by all this? Know well that love was what he meant. Who showed you this? Love. What did he show? Love. Why did he show it to you? For love.[2]

Wonderful.

---

2. Julian of Norwich, *Revelations of Divine Love* 86 (long text; Spearing, 179).

"Something Else"

Yet in our day and age, we need to guard against sentimentalized reductions of what this means—cut-down-to-size versions of what is meant when we say things like "God" and "love." I call such reductions a false gospel of "niceness." It's one of those feel-good quick fixes that do us no good in the long run. It confuses God's love for us for some sort of mere infatuation. But here's the situation: neither we ourselves, nor the circumstances in which we find ourselves, are entirely all that "nice." To say the least.

We needed something else, other than mere infatuation; we needed vastly more than a "god" who had a mere *crush* on us. Such a "god" isn't there. What we needed was a truly loving and disruptive *intervention*—a fierce, determined, effective, and *saving* love—from the God who really *is* there. God's love could no more be indifferent to the reality of our plight than a loving parent could be "OK" with their child's devastating illness—or their child's captivity in some horrific addiction.

So: to any now who may be burdened with some deep-down, uncomfortable dissatisfaction with all the false comforts and false gospels—to any who may be distressed by some new sense of an unbridgeable gap between what is and what ought to be—I offer this: that such dissatisfaction, and such distress, just might be from the early breathings of the regenerating Spirit, early signs that the righteous God of unbounded love has something *infinitely better* in store—the unreachable, and perhaps unsuspected, heart's desire that if we've been seeking at all, we've been seeking all along. And, thanks be, that's what God gives.

> "herefore, since we are justified by faith, we have peace with God through our Lord Jesus Christ, through whom we have obtained access to this grace in which we stand. (Rom 5:1–2a)

Now it all begins.

Meanwhile, I might suggest far-more-appropriate "daily affirmations" for the journey.

Here's one, taken from the writings of Augustine:

> God did not indeed extend his mercy to us because we knew him, but in order that we might know him; nor was it because we were upright in heart, but that we might become so, that he extended to us his righteousness, whereby he justifies the ungodly . . . 'But why,' says one, 'is not the grace of God given according to our merits?' I answer, Because God is merciful.[3]

---

3. Augustine, *On the Spirit and the Letter*, 11 [VII] and *On the Gift of Perseverance* 16 [VIII] (*NPNF1* 5:87, 531).

"Receive the Kingdom of God as a Little Child"

All Saints Church, Columbia Falls, Montana

Year B, Proper 22: Mark 10:15
Sunday, October 6, 2024
Valediction

> Verily I say unto you, Whosoever shall not receive the kingdom of God as a little child, he shall not enter therein.

SOME MIGHT BE TEMPTED to think that what Jesus said here is just a bit of genial sentimentality. It isn't. Instead, it offers us a profound challenge but also, an astounding promise.

Right away, however, we ought to underscore the difference between *childlikeness*, which our Lord enjoins here as a condition for receiving the kingdom of God, and—on the other hand—*childishness*, which is immaturity in relation to where someone ought to be in terms of age-appropriate development as a person.

Of course, these—childlikeness and childishness—are extraordinarily different! If one is five, or ten, or fifteen, and one's development is apt for that respective age, well and good. But if one is thirty, and one is still carrying on at the maturity level of a five, ten, or fifteen year old, we have a serious problem.

This is fully consistent with what Paul says in his First Letter to the Corinthians, chapter thirteen, verse eleven:

> When I was a child, I spake as a child, I understood as a child, I thought as a child: but when I became a man, I put away childish things.

"Receive the Kingdom of God as a Little Child"

Jesus is speaking about something entirely different. Childlikeness is both the *condition* and also the *disposition* of one's person that are an essential part of following him. But—please take note—our Lord is not enjoining childlikeness generally, in all of our present spheres of life. Rather, he is indicating it, specifically, in relation to God—and in relation to one's participation in God's kingdom.

So, in relation to God and God's kingdom, what are the condition and the disposition to which Jesus is calling us?

First, let's ponder condition—or, we might say, the issue of *status*.

Put simply, especially in the ancient world, children had *no* status! Theirs was a position of utter vulnerability. In the midst of all the issues of this present life, as we grow up, we develop all sorts of protective layers around ourselves. By these, we seek to minimize danger and hold risk at bay. And in the realm of the flesh, to a significant extent, this is unavoidable—even sometimes necessary. This is a fallen world.

But before God, it will not do! We may not hold up all our "stuff" before him, as some sort of protective shield. However, as we "grow up," becoming vulnerable before anything, or anyone, seems to get harder and harder, doesn't it? Maybe even, in human terms, impossible, requiring nothing less than the intervention of the Spirit. But as Jesus calls, the Spirit intervenes, and the impossible demand—amazingly—is actualized.

> And when Jesus had called the people *unto him* with his disciples also, he said unto them, "Whosoever will come after me, let him deny himself, and take up his cross, and follow me. For whosoever will save his life shall lose it; but whosoever shall lose his life for my sake and the gospel's, the same shall save it. For what shall it profit a man, if he shall gain the whole world, and lose his own soul?" (Mark 8:34–36)

This involves releasing our grip—that desperate grip—on our prior earthly "status." We must release it, especially, as the means by which we had sought to define, understand, and—somehow—try to protect ourselves. In worldly terms, releasing this grip is not easy. It's hard, whether our prior condition was comparatively easy or challenging!

Whether we liked the world "before" or not, it was the world we knew, and in its predictability, we had some means of "managing" it, at least psychically.

But following Jesus means laying aside the idols of fleshly management and control. The real freedom that the Lord gives will mean—among other things—that our precious rings of power will be cast into the fires of Mount Doom.

Yes, to be sure,

> With men *it is* impossible; but not with God: for with God all things are possible. (Mark 10:27)

We fall all-too-much in love with our worldly status, don't we? This is true, whether this be a status of privilege, or even one of "victimhood." But for those in Christ, neither of these will now serve as the interpretive framework of our life.

Childlikeness, in him, means being undefendedly present to him in whatever condition we find ourselves. And it also means, more and more, as we grow in faith, that we will be present in this broken world, as his people: both in our being and in our doing.

Now, going on to the disposition—or, we might say, the *attitude*—involved in receiving God's kingdom.

Yes, this is a world of disillusionment. But in Christ, we are summoned once again to the attitude, before God, of childlike wonder and of delight. Our protective layers are set aside that we may behold the excellence, the surpassing worth, and—ultimately—the beauty of God. And the people who now see so differently—who see as they were meant to see—first God then, in him, everything else—make more difference than they know! That most certainly is part of the plan.

Christians, I am convinced, are to be part of the godly re-enchantment of the world.

These days, this is a profoundly countercultural endeavor. The spirit of the age is cynical: know-it-all, snarky, and oppressively self-referential. Its mode of discourse is thoroughly ironic. We find ourselves bereft of wonder. These days, it takes a great deal of courage to be surprised by anything.[1] Our society seems determined to hustle even our young people out of all childlikeness—and usher them, as early as possible, into the disenchanted kingdom.

But whose needs are really being served in such a hustle?

> Whosoever shall not receive the kingdom of God as a little child, he shall not enter therein.

---

1. Allusions, of course, both indirect and direct, to Lewis's *Surprised by Joy*. Lewis himself drew the title from the poem by William Wordsworth.

"Receive the Kingdom of God as a Little Child"

Those at all familiar with my preaching know that it's only a matter of time before C. S. Lewis gets quoted. Here's an excerpt from one of his essays that's relevant to the topic at hand:

> Critics who treat "adult" as a term of approval, instead of as a merely descriptive term, cannot be adult themselves. To be concerned about being grown up, to admire the grown up because it is grown up, to blush at the suspicion of being childish; these things are the marks of childhood and adolescence. And in childhood and adolescence they are, in moderation, healthy symptoms. Young things ought to want to grow. But to carry on into middle life or even into early manhood this concern about being adult is a mark of really arrested development: When I was ten I read fairy tales in secret and would have been ashamed if I had been found doing so. Now that I am fifty I read them openly. When I became a man I put away childish things, including the fear of childishness and the desire to be very grown up.[2]

Godly wonder and delight: these two do go together, but it should be stressed that they don't of necessity initially arrive right away, at the same time. Specifically, the delight in God may come later for us. After all, in the here-and-now, the realm of godly re-enchantment certainly has its perils! It isn't always "feel-good." It isn't entirely "safe," as we presently, in fleshly terms, might define safety. The beatific vision—or perhaps, even bits of the beatific vision—usually come to us only after a rather demanding passage.

But for those in Christ Jesus, we may be sure that the vision will be given. And we may be sure that those, in him, will surely be held in his saving purpose: in all his competence and in all his good will.

> All that the Father giveth me shall come to me; and anyone that cometh to me I will in no wise cast out ... My sheep hear my voice, and I know them, and they follow me: and I give unto them eternal life; and they shall never perish, neither shall any *man* pluck them out of my hand. (John 6:37; 10:27–28)

So, it's not a matter of being so very anxious about working up in ourselves exactly the right kind of attitude, in order that we might then be received into God's kingdom. It's about the kind of attitude—the kind of disposition—that goes along with being so received. In faith, it's to Christ that we look, not to ourselves.

---

2. "On Three Ways of Writing for Children," in Lewis, *On Stories*, 34.

I'll risk offering an example, such as it is, of what we've been considering from my own life story. But—in addition to its use here as a modest illustration—perhaps also might serve as an invitation to each of you to "consider your own call" in faith (1 Cor 1:26 NRSV).

OK: my first year of college; fifty-two years ago.

I'd been telling myself, for some time, that I was "through" with Christianity. But I also knew—increasingly and to my great distress at the time—that this just wasn't so. I had recently had some Bible quoted at me and decided to read it for myself.

I didn't own a copy of the Bible at the time, so I decided to get one at the used bookstore across from the campus. I went to its religion section, saw a lineup of Bibles, and selected an old, black-covered, red-edged King James. The price was right: 75¢. So—dearly hoping that no one that I knew would see me—I took it to the checkout counter and made the purchase.

That night, back at home, I dug in. Years before, I'd heard Scripture in church and done some reading of it at home, as part of my preparation for Confirmation. But this was the first time, personally, I had followed the bidding to "take up and read" at a much deeper level.[3]

As Christianity was the heart of my "problem," I went to the New Testament—its first book, Matthew's Gospel. I read Matthew straight through, in one, very attentive reading. This attention wasn't a choice on my part; it was—somehow—just summoned.

The experience was moving, disturbing—in fact, overwhelming. Whether I liked what I was reading or not—whether I agreed with it or not, believed it or not—was irrelevant. Somehow, unlikely as it was, I had given it an undefended reading, and through this, on every page, an utter, inescapable sense of the authenticity of Jesus broke through to me. That night, I had been reduced—though I might now say, had been *restored*—to at least a measure of childlikeness.

I was still a long way off from being claimed in faith. But this Christ was now, even more, a factor to be dealt with. But even then, I knew that I was not really in charge of the process; I knew that I wasn't so much doing the dealing but that I was *being dealt with*. Flannery O'Connor wrote of the American South being "Christ-haunted."[4] My soul was increasingly Christ-haunted territory.

---

3. See Augustine, *Confessions* 8.12.29 (Chadwick, 152).

4. "The Grotesque in Southern Literature" and "The Catholic Novelist in the Protestant South," in O'Connor, *Collected Works*, 818, 861.

"Receive the Kingdom of God as a Little Child"

This isn't the place to relate the rest of my conversion story. Suffice to say that—for a good while yet—I struggled, evaded, and tried so very hard to figure things out. Thanks be, though, there came a time when—from beyond myself—a resolution, and gracious claiming, came to me. Surprised by joy,[5] I might even say: surprised by the Joy of the risen and eternally living Christ.

Needless to say, any conversion to Christ is an initiation into an ongoing process. As we grow in him, in our long journey, we will have repeated opportunities to cease from our evasions, to lay aside our distancing mechanisms—and once again, to become vulnerable before him.

All sorts of stuff in us—and all sorts of stuff around us—will do everything it can to have us pull back. It will do everything it can to tell us to avoid such risky exposure, to play it "safe" and "hedge our bets." "Don't be foolish," it says! Yet this so-called "foolishness" is really the greatest of all wisdom.

And—astoundingly!—"for us and for our salvation,"[6] this God, in the Person of his incarnate Son, Jesus, became *first in line* in the path of utter vulnerability, to the point of "death, even the death of the cross" (Phil 2:8). There, on our behalf, exposed on the cross, he took upon himself the utter negation of all fleshly status—and there, too, in terrible wonder, he accomplished the victory of God and the redemption of our souls.

Just how far did he go to get to us? All the way. Righteousness bore our iniquity. Beauty bore our ugliness. Perfection bore our woundedness. The One Who Is Life died our death. Christ—blessedness himself—"redeemed us . . . having become a curse for us" (Gal 3:13 RSV). In the words of Gregory of Nazianzus' classic affirmation:

> That which He has not assumed He has not healed, but that which is united to His Godhead is saved.[7]

He came all the way *to* us and *for* us.

Therefore, "come unto [him]," the living victor over sin and death. Come unto him, "who is and who was and who is to come" (Matt 11:28; Rev 1:8).

---

5. Again an allusion to Lewis, *Surprised by Joy*.

6. The Nicene Creed, in *Book of Common Prayer*, 326.

7. Gregory of Nazianzus, *To Cledonius* (NPNF2 8:440). See also "First Letter to Cledonius," 5, in Gregory of Nazianzus, *On God and Christ*, 158.

> Verily I say unto you, Whosoever shall not receive the kingdom of
> God as a little child, he shall not enter therein.

To be sure, all sorts of stuff in us, and all sorts of stuff around us—the worst, and also, what we might deem the best and most important in our "oh-so-grown-up, but not grown-up" life—may wail at the utter difficulty of doing so.

But really, by the grace of him who calls, it is the simplest thing in the world.

Biographical Note

"The Spirit lifted me up, and brought me to the east gate of the house of the Lord."

(Ezek 11:1a)

ADAM LINTON WAS BORN on October 11, 1954, a native of the San Francisco Bay Area. Sausalito is his hometown. On November 11, 1962, along with his father and sister, he was baptized at Christ Church Episcopal, Sausalito. On June 6, 1965, also at Christ Church, he was confirmed. He and his family remained active there until 1967. In the autumn of 1972, he began attending the Orthodox Church and was received into its membership in the spring of 1974. He returned to the fellowship of the Episcopal Church in 1996.

He and his wife, Lori, were married on July 17, 1977. They have five children and six grandchildren.

He is a graduate of the College of Marin, Kentfield, California; Saint Tikhon's Orthodox Theological Seminary, South Canaan, Pennsylvania (1980); and Gordon-Conwell Theological Seminary, South Hamilton, Massachusetts (Master of Divinity, 1990).

He was ordained as a priest in the Orthodox Church in America on October 10, 1980, and served parishes in Colorado and Massachusetts, as well as serving as an active-duty chaplain in the United States Navy and then in church administration.

On October 16, 1997, his priestly orders were received in the Episcopal Church (Bishop Frank Griswold, Diocese of Chicago), and thereafter he served parishes in Illinois, Utah, and Massachusetts, and additionally on standing committee (Utah) and as a deputy to general convention (2006). He retired in 2019. He and Lori then relocated to Northwest Montana. Thereafter he continued to serve occasionally and on a part-time basis through 2024.

Bibliography

Auden, W. H. *For the Time Being: A Christmas Oratorio.* New York: Random House, 1944. Reprint, edited by Alan Jacobs, Princeton: Princeton University Press, 2013.
Augustine. *Concerning the City of God Against the Pagans.* Translated by Henry Bettenson. London: Penguin, 1984.
———. *Confessions.* Translated by Henry Chadwick, Oxford: Oxford University Press, 1991.
———. *Essential Sermons.* Translated by Edmond Hill. Hyde Park, NY: New City, 2007.
———. *A Select Library of the Nicene and Post-Nicene Fathers (First Series): Volume V, Saint Augustine, Anti-Pelagian Writings.* Translated by Peter Holmes and Robert Ernest Wallis. Edited by Philip Schaff. Reprint, Grand Rapids: Eerdmans, 1971.
———. *The Trinity (De Trinitate).* Translated by Edmond Hill. Hyde Park, NY: New City, 1991.
Arnold, Matthew. *Dover Beach and Other Poems.* Mineoloa, NY: Dover, 2012.
Barfield, Owen. *Poetic Diction: A Study in Meaning.* London: Faber and Gwyer, 1928. Reprint, Hanover, CT: Wesleyan University Press, 1973.
Barth, Karl. *Christ and Adam: Man and Humanity in Romans 5.* Translated by T. A. Small. New York: Harper & Brothers, 1956. Reprint, Eugene, OR: Wipf and Stock, 2004.
———. *Church Dogmatics.* Translated by G. W. Bromiley et al., edited by G. W. Bromiley and T. F. Torrance. Study Edition. London: T & T Clark, 2009.
———. *The Epistle to the Romans.* Translated from the Sixth Edition by Edwyn C. Hoskins. Oxford: Oxford University Press, 1933.
———. *Homiletics.* Translated by G. W. Bromiley and Donald E. Daniels. Louisville: Westminster/John Knox, 1991.
———. *The Word of God and the Word of Man.* Translated by Douglas Horton. London: Hodder and Stoughton, 1928. Reprint, Gloucester, MA: Peter Smith, 1978.
The Book of Common Prayer. New York: Seabury, 1979. [Amended 2006 to include the Revised Common Lectionary.]
Bunyan, John. *Grace Abounding to the Chief of Sinners.* Edited by W. R. Owens. London: Penguin, 1987.
———. *The Pilgrim's Process.* Edited by W. R. Owens. Oxford: Oxford University Press, 2003.
Burke, Edmond. *Reflections on the Revolution in France and Other Writings.* Edited by Jesse Norman. New York: Alfred A. Knopf, 2015.
Calvin, John. *Institutes of the Christian Religion.* Translated by Ford Lewis Battles. Edited by John T. McNeill. Philadelphia: Westminster, 1960.

BIBLIOGRAPHY

Chrysostom, John. *A Select Library of the Nicene and Post-Nicene Fathers (First Series): Volume XIII, Saint Chrysostom: Homilies on Galatians, Ephesians, Philippians, Colossians, Thessalonians, Timothy, Titus, and Philemon*. Edited by Philip Schaff. Reprint, Grand Rapids, MA: Eerdmans, 1956.

Concordia: The Lutheran Confessions: A Reader's Edition of the Book of Concord (Second Edition). Edited by Paul Timothy McCain. St. Louis: Concordia, 2005.

Conrad, Joseph. *The Secret Sharer and Other Stories*. Edited by John G. Peters. New York: W. W. Norton, 2015.

———. *Youth/Heart of Darkness/The End of the Tether*. Edited by John Lyon. London: Penguin, 1995.

Dickinson, Emily. *The Complete Poems of Emily Dickinson*. Edited by Thomas H. Johnson. Boston: Little, Brown and Company, 1960.

Donne, John. *The Complete English Poems*. Edited by A. J. Smith. London: Penguin, 1971.

Dostoevsky, Fyodor. *The Brothers Karamazov*. Translated by Constance Garnett. Revised by Ralph E. Matlaw. New York: W. W. Norton, 1976.

———. *The Brothers Karamazov: A Novel in Four Parts with Epilogue*. Translated by Richard Pevear and Larissa Volokhonsky. New York: Farrar, Straus and Giroux, 1990.

———. *Crime and Punishment: A Novel in Six Parts with Epilogue*. Translated by Richard Pevear and Larissa Volokhonsky. New York: Vintage, 1992.

Gregory of Nazianzus. *Festal Orations*. Translated by Nonna Verna Harrison. Crestwood, NY: St. Vladimir's Seminary Press, 2008.

———. *On God and Christ: The Five Theological Orations and Two Letters to Cledonius*. Translated by Lionel Wickham and Frederick Williams. Crestwood, NY: St. Vladimir's Seminary Press, 2002.

———. *A Select Library of the Nicene and Post-Nicene Fathers (Second Series): Volume VII, S. Cyrill of Jerusalem, S. Gregory Nazianzen*. Edited by Philip Schaff and Henry Wace. Reprint, Grand Rapids: Eerdmans, 1983.

Gregory of Nyssa. *Gregory of Nyssa: Homilies on the Song of Songs*. Translated by Richard A. Norris. Atlanta: Society of Biblical Literature, 2012.

Hapgood, Isabel Florence. *Service Book of the Holy Orthodox-Catholic Apostolic Church, Revised Edition*. New York: Association Press, 1922. Reprint, Englewood, NJ: Antiochian Orthodox Christian Archdiocese, 1996.

Herbert, George. *The Complete English Poems*. Edited by John Tobin. London: Penguin, 1991.

Hooker, Richard. *The Works of Mr. Richard Hooker*. 7th ed. Arranged by John Keble. Revised by R. W. Church and F. Paget. Oxford: Clarendon, 1888.

Hopkins, Gerard Manley. *Poems and Prose of Gerard Manley Hopkins*. Edited by W. H. Gardner. London: Penguin, 1953.

The Hymnal 1982. New York: Church Publishing Incorporated, 1985.

Isaac the Syrian. *The Ascetical Homilies of Saint Isaac the Syrian, Revised Second Edition*. Translated by Holy Transfiguration Monastery. Boston: Holy Transfiguration Monastery, 2011.

———. *Isaac of Ninevah (Isaac the Syrian): 'The Second Part', Chapters IV-XLI*. Translated by Sebastian Block. Leuven: Peeters, 1995.

Iverson, Kelly R. *Gentiles in the Gospel of Mark: 'Even the Dogs Under the Table Eat the Children's Crumbs.'* London: T&T Clark, 2007.

Julian of Norwich. *Revelations of Divine Love: Short Text and Long Text*. Translated by Elizabeth Spearing. London: Penguin, 1998.

Bibliography

Levine, Amy-Jill. *Short Stories by Jesus: The Enigmatic Parables of a Controversial Rabbi.* New York: HarperCollins, 2014.

Lewis, C. S. *An Experiment in Criticism.* Cambridge: Cambridge University Press, 1961.

———. *The Great Divorce: A Dream.* London: Geoffrey Bless [Centenary], 1946. Reprint, New York: HarperCollins, 2001.

———. *The Lion, the Witch and the Wardrobe.* London: Geoffrey Bless, 1950. Reprint, New York: HarperCollins, 1991.

———. *On Stories and Other Essays on Literature.* Edited by Walter Hooper. New York: Harcourt, Brace & Company [Harvest], 1982.

———. *The Silver Chair.* London: Geoffrey Bless, 1953. Reprint, New York: Harper Collins, 1991.

———. *Surprised by Joy: The Shape of My Early Life.* London: Geoffrey Bless, 1955. Reprint, New York: Harcourt [Harvest], 1966.

Lincoln, Abraham. *Abraham Lincoln: Speeches and Writings, 1859–1865.* New York: Library of America, 1989.

Louth, Andrew, ed. *Early Christian Writings: The Apostolic Fathers.* Rev. ed. Translated by Maxwell Staniforth. London: Penguin, 1987.

Luther, Martin. *Commentary on Galatians.* Translated by Erasmus Middleton. London: Harrison Trust, 1850. Reprint, Grand Rapids: Kegel, 1979.

Malamud, Bernard. *The Complete Stories.* Edited by Robert Giroux. New York: Farrar, Straus and Groux [Noonday], 1997.

O'Connor, Flannery. *Collected Works.* New York: Library of America, 1988.

Otto, Rudolf. *The Idea of the Holy: An Inquiry into the Non-rational Factor in the Idea of the Divine and its Relation to the Rational.* Translated by John W. Harvey. London: Oxford University Press, 1923.

Rutledge, Fleming. *By the Word Worked: Encountering the Power of Biblical Preaching.* Waco, TX: Baylor University Press, 2024.

———. *The Crucifixion: Understanding the Death of Jesus Christ.* Grand Rapids: Eerdmans, 2015.

———. *Not Ashamed of the Gospel: Sermons from Paul's Letter to the Romans.* Grand Rapids: Eerdmans, 2007.

Saint-Exupéry, Antoine de. *Wind, Sand and Stars.* Translated by Lewis Galantiére. New York: Reynal and Hitchcock, 1939. Reprint, New York: Harcourt [Harvest], 1992.

A Select Library of the Nicene and Post-Nicene Fathers (Second Series): Volume XIV, The Seven Ecumenical Councils. Edited by Philip Schaff and Henry Wace. Reprint, Grand Rapids: Eerdmans, 1991.

Spurgeon, C. H. *All of Grace: An Earnest Word for Those Who Are Seeking Salvation by the Lord Jesus Christ.* London: Passmore and Alabaster, 1886. Reprint, Chicago: Moody, 2010.

Tolkien, J. R. R. *The Lord of the Rings: 50th Anniversary Edition.* Boston/New York: Houghton Mifflin, 2004.

———. *Tree and Leaf: Including the Poem Mythopoeia.* London: George Allen & Unwin, 1964. Reprint, London: HarperCollins, 2001.

Willard, Dallas. *The Allure of Gentleness: Defending the Faith in the Manner of Jesus.* New York: HarperCollins, 2013.

Yeats, W. B. *The Collected Poems of W. B. Yeats: A New Edition.* Edited by Richard J. Finneran. New York: Macmillan [Collier], 1983.

Scripture Index

Genesis

1:1	6
1:4	6
1:31	7
1:27; 5:2	24
12:3	71
18:1–8	24
22:1–18	10–13
22:2	12
22:14	13

Exodus

20:1–17	122
20:2–3	128–33, 130

Deuteronomy

6:4	22
6:13	109, 112
6:16	113
8:2	11
8:3	112
21:23	65
30:15–20	119–24

1 Kings

19:12	75

Psalms

1	119–24, 121
22:1	65
46	113
56:8	35
91:11–12	112
104:24	48
111:10	48
118:24	49

Proverbs

9:10	48

Isaiah

30:29	105
40:21	105
44:6	93
53:5	127
53:6	136
58:11	78

Jeremiah

17:9	130
23:6	113

Ezekiel

11:1a	145
47:1–12	75–80, 78

Daniel

5:27	xxiii

Joel

2:32	86

Jonah

2:1–9	1–4
2:1–2	2
2:3–4	1
2:5, 9	4
2:6–7	3
2:8	3

Matthew

4:9–10	109
6:24	83
6:25	108
7:13, 14	xiii, 120
11:28–30	121
11:28–29	xiii
11:28	66, 143
13:45–46	41–45
14:22–33	1–4
15:21–28	68
16:18	xx
25:37, 40	29
26:22	64
27:45, 50–52	126
27:46	65

Mark

1:15	71, 72
3:7–8	71
4:35—5:20	70
5:21–43	96–100
5:27	100
5:36	99
5:41	98
5:43	99
6:30–44	72
7:24–37	68–74
7:27–28	72
7:28	71
7:34	72
8:1–10	72
8:27–38	51–56
8:29–30	51
8:31	52
8:34–35	52, 56
8:34–36	139
9:9	46
10:15	138
10:23b–27	106–10
10:24b–27	108
10:27	140
12:29	22
15:43	65
16:1–8	46–50
16:6	49
16:8	49

Luke

2:49	75, 80
4:1–13	111–14
4:1–3	111–12
4:4–7	112
4:8–11	112
4:12	113
4:22–30	57–63
4:22, 28–29a	57
9:51–62	115–18
10:20	117
10:42	42
13:24	120
14:25–33	119
14:25–26	119
14:27	121
18:11	132
22:14—23:56	64–67
23:18	65
23:23	67
23:33–43	125–27
23:42	127

John

1:1–14	xii
1:3b	3
1:5	98
2:21	78
4:5–42	134, 135
6:35ff	72
6:37	141

Scripture Index

6:46	24
6:51	77
6:68	xviii
7:37–39	75–80, 77–78
8:44	114
10:10	xiii, 4, 114
10:27–28	141
11:1–44	96
12:32	65
12:32–33	127
14:6	15
15:26	23
19:19	65
19:30	120
19:34	78

Acts

1:11	90
26:14	xv

Romans

3:8	81
3:23	88
3:23–24	135
4:3–5, 23–25; 5:1–11	134–37
4:4–5; 5:6, 8, 10	135–36
4:17	xii, 136
4:19	11
5:1	38, 135
5:1–2a	137
5:1–11	37–40
5:3–5	40
5:6	38
5:8–9	39
5:15–19	5–9, 6
5:20	xxi, 9, 89
6:1–4, 15–19	82
6:2	84
6:3	10, 52
6:11	85
6:12–23	81–85
6:13	82
6:23	81
8:14–17a	25
8:33	135
10:6–13	86–89
10:6	86
10:8b–13	111
10:9	80
10:9–10	113
10:13	86
10:17	105

1 Corinthians

1:18–23	51
1:21	vi
1:26	142
2:2	63, 136
6:19	78
11:26	52
11:27–29	8
12:3–13	75–80
12:3	75–76
12:4–7	79
13:1–13	57–63
13:1–3	58
13:7	62
13:9–13	63
13:11	138
13:12	29, 93
15:45	7
15:57	84

2 Corinthians

1:20	85
4:7	22
11:14	83

Galatians

2:20	53
3:13	64–67, 65, 143
3:26	105
5:1	117
5:13–17	115
5:22–25	116
6:2	60
6:7–16	115–18
6:7–8	115, 116
6:14	53
6:15b	63, 117

Ephesians

2:14	94
2:19–22	79
4:13	63
6:12	76

Philippians

1:9	133
2:5b-8	44
2:8	130, 136
2:12b-13	116
3:4b-14	128–33
3:7–9	128, 131
3:10,12–14	132–33
4:7	xiii

Colossians

1:11–20	125–27
1:13, 19–20	xviii, 126
1:15–17	xii
1:24	vi

1 Timothy

1:15–17	18
1:15–16	14–19
1:15	14
2:4	109
3:15	xx
6:19	85, 114

2 Timothy

3:16	xi

Titus

2:11	3

Hebrews

1:1–4; 2:5–12	26–30, 101–5
1:1–2	26, 101
1:2–3a	xii
1:3	27, 103
2:9	27, 103
2:17	103
4:12–16	106–10
4:12	xii, 109
4:14	108
4:15	103, 111
4:16	109
7:25	104, 106
10:10	101, 107, 110
11:12	11
11:32	xxiv
12:1	104, 129
12:2	3, 103, 110
13:8	102, 107
13:12–13	67
13:14	133

James

1:20	118

1 Peter

1:18–20	xviii
2:4–5	79

2 Peter

1:20	xiv
3:8–15a	90–95
3:8–10	91
3:11, 14, 15	95
3:13	92
3:14	94

1 John

1:1	22
3:2	93
4:8b	63

Jude

3	xv

Scripture Index

Revelation

1:8	93, 143
2:7	32
3:14	85, 114
7:9–17	31–36
7:9–11	33
7:12	36
7:13–14	34
7:17	35
13:8	xviii, 127
19:11	85, 114
21:5	33, 55
21:6; 22:3	93
22:20	93

www.ingramcontent.com/pod-product-compliance
Lightning Source LLC
Chambersburg PA
CBHW050811160426
43192CB00010B/1722